Joseph Itiel

A Consumer's Guide
to Male Hustlers

D0226134

Pre-publication
REVIEWS,
COMMENTARIES,
EVALUATIONS . . .

"**J**oseph Itiel's guide is witty and wise—a delight to read. Copiously illustrated with anecdotes from his astonishingly vast experience, it entertains and informs with clear and practical advice on taking control of one's own sex life. Noteworthy is the author's distinction between female prostitutes and male hustlers, whom he calls 'independent contractors.' If you are thinking of sampling the world of hustlers, this book is a must. Even if you are sexually experienced, you will enjoy comparing notes, and I guarantee you will pick up some pointers along the way. By the way, hustlers can pick up some good tips here too."

Hubert Kennedy, PhD
Research Associate,
Center for Research and Education in Sexuality,
San Francisco State University

"**J**oseph Itiel's book *A Consumer's Guide to Male Hustlers* is exactly that—an informative 'how-to book' in the delicate art of sex selection on demand. American Express comes to mind: 'Don't bring 'em home without it.' "

Dr. J. Davis Mannino
Psychologist; Author,
Sexually Speaking

A Consumer's Guide to Male Hustlers

HAWORTH Gay & Lesbian Studies
John P. De Cecco, PhD
Editor in Chief

A Consumer's Guide to Male Hustlers

Joseph Itiel

Harrington Park Press
An Imprint of The Haworth Press, Inc.
New York • London

Published by

Harrington Park Press, an imprint of The Haworth Press, Inc., 10 Alice Street, Binghamton, NY 13904-1580

Cover design by Marylouise E. Doyle.

The Library of Congress has cataloged the hardcover edition of this book as:

Itiel, Joseph.
   A consumer's guide to male hustlers / Joseph Itiel.
      p. cm.
Includes index.
ISBN 0-7890-0596-4 (alk. paper)
   1. Male prostitution. 2. Sex instruction for gay men. 3. Gay men—Sexual behavior. I. Title.
HQ76.1.I86 1998
306.74'3—dc21
                                                                   98–8164
                                                                     CIP

ISBN 1-56023-947-6 (pbk.)

CONTENTS

ABOUT THE AUTHOR

More than forty years ago, Joseph Itiel decided to bring under control his gay erotic instincts. He traveled to Rishikesh, India, where he studied Yoga in an ashram. Yoga toned his body but left its sexual needs unanswered. He then renounced sex completely. This made him feel irritable, preoccupied, and thwarted. He returned to the world of the flesh, and after exploring various paths in many countries, found his answer in a unique gay lifestyle. He meets with hustlers regularly, establishing mutually beneficial relations with them. He makes his home in San Francisco, CA.

Acknowledgments

My first thanks must go to Steve Kotz, who urged me to write this book and then helped me prepare the manuscript. He made invaluable suggestions to assist me in dealing with sensitive issues. It was he who encouraged me to share myself fully with my readers. Thanks also to Howard Curtis and David Klein, who read the manuscript. Their insightful comments and observations were incorporated into the work. For many years Vicki Newton has urged me to persevere in my writing in the face of rejections and indifference by agents and publishers. When I all but gave up, her support kept me going.

All characters in this book are real. However, I have taken great pains to change not only their names, but also their physical and ethnic descriptions, as well as their places of origin and the work they do. Consequently, any similarity to living or dead persons is purely coincidental.

Also by Joseph Itiel

Financial Well-Being Through Self-Hypnosis

The Franz Document

Philippine Diary: A Gay Guide to the Philippines

De Onda: A Gay Guide to Mexico and Its People

Pura Vida: A Gay and Lesbian Guide to Costa Rica

Introduction

If you are a gay man practicing abstinence, or are in a strict monogamous relationship, this book is not for you. Likewise, if you are content to go to bars and return home horny and alone, or spend untold hours in a sex club without scoring, you do not need this book.

The purpose of this work is to acquaint readers who have a vigorous sexual appetite with a resource available in the gay community that is often shunned or used inappropriately. It is not my intention to romanticize or glamorize hustlers. As in my previous guidebooks, I want to share with readers my personal experiences and observations.

My dealings with hustlers, over a period of some thirty-five years and in many countries, have been (with a few notable exceptions!) very satisfactory. In addition to good sex, I have also developed emotional relationships with a number of hustlers. The very nature of our relationships have kept our deepening emotional involvement under control, which is a good thing for all concerned.

Control is a very important issue for both hustlers and their clients. I will explore the many facets of this issue in this book. For the moment, let me say that by assuming control over my sexual fortunes I have escaped the profound mood swings associated with the uncertain results of cruising.

My goal is to dispel many erroneous notions about hustlers. Among the many issues I will explore are:

- Are sex-for-money arrangements exploitative?
- Can there be emotional involvement between clients and hustlers?
- Can only the wealthy afford hustlers?
- Aren't hustlers likely carriers of sexually transmitted diseases?
- How dangerous is the hustling scene?
- Why do hustlers hustle?
- Are male and female prostitution just two sides of the same coin?
- What are the differences between street hustlers, models (sometimes called escorts), and masseurs?

There are a number of legal issues associated with hustling. They will be discussed at length in the appropriate places. For the moment, I would like to address one aspect: This book refers only to men who have reached the age of majority and can make their own decisions, free from physical or psychological coercion. I DO NOT ADVOCATE OR PROMOTE CHILD PROSTITUTION.

As a travel writer I have discussed situations in which gay travelers run into minors, of both sexes, who solicit business aggressively. At times, it is impossible to ascertain the true age of the people accosting them. My advice has always been the same: "When in doubt regarding the age of your prospective partner, just say NO." The person whose age you question is replaceable with another hustler. Underage hustlers are a major hassle you do not need!

This is a book about a sex resource rather than about finding love. However, seeing hustlers can facilitate establishing a love relationship because it makes dating easier. It takes less determination not to seek immediate sexual gratification on a date after having had a good session with a hustler. Regular sessions with hustlers as an emotional and libidinal sedative is a subject I shall discuss at length.

Probably the most common complaint in gay life is that (other) people play games. Not infrequently, both players wind up the losers in these games. With hustlers, if you know what your are doing, and your partner is cooperative, both parties will be winners. My goal is to help readers achieve win/win experiences with their hustlers.

Chapter 1

How It Began

This is a book about hustlers. The biographical information in this chapter is not essential to the subject of this work. Here I want to share with readers my sexual evolution—from haphazard cruising to planned sex with hustlers; to explain how, at the age of twenty-six, I discovered the benefits of hiring hustlers; and how it was possible for me, earning an average salary, to pay for their services. If you are not interested in my personal history, feel free to skip this chapter.

My first homosexual encounter took place in New York City. I arrived there in 1950, as a student, at the age of nineteen. Until then I had lived in Tel Aviv, Israel. Even though I had known from a very early age that I was gay, the thought of performing homosexual acts led to a feeling of profound anxiety. In my four years in New York, I had only two such experiences.[1] Both were far from ideal.

After graduating from college, I moved to Toronto, Ontario, and entered law school. The pressure of my studies increased my sexual urge. We took up criminal law in the first semester, and I became acutely aware of the severe penalties for indulging in a homosexual act. In 1955, homosexuality was still very much illegal in Canada, though the law was not enforced rigidly. But I could not stop myself from seeking sex partners.

I started cruising the parks in Toronto. It was wintertime and bitterly cold. Very few people, straight or gay, were out and about. Eventually, in the spring, I discovered the one cruise-worthy location in Toronto, aptly named Queen's Park. There I managed, occasionally and with great trepidation, to make contact with fellow cruisers.

In those days Toronto was, by and large, an Anglo-Saxon city. Alas, fair people have never appealed to me sexually. From boyhood on, I have been attracted to darker and, in my eyes, more exotic men. I remember vividly that in my early teens I had acquired a lot of travel books, with photographs of people the world over. I would stare endlessly at photos of African, American Indian, and Asian men, and fantasize lustfully. For whatever reasons, I paid no attention to the men who looked like myself.

Because of my sexual preferences, I was not particularly attracted to most of the men I saw at Queen's Park. The very few I cared for did not fancy me. The men I finally got it on with, after endless cruising, were of little interest to me physically. I comforted myself that having sex with them was better than nothing. For practical reasons, I tried to meet some of my less-than-ideal contacts on a regular basis but this rarely worked out. None of the people I had met ever talked about becoming lovers or even boyfriends.

I did not know about gay bars until much later. Even if I had known about them earlier, my life would not have improved. In those days, in Ontario, only the bartender was permitted to move drinks from one spot to another. Also, patrons were not allowed to stand while holding drinks. When I stumbled, finally, upon a mainly gay bar in Toronto, I felt like a prisoner in it. For me, cruising the parks was the lesser of two evils.

By the end of my first year at law school, there were too many pressures on me to allow me to pursue my studies. My instructors repeated over and over again how we, as lawyers, would become "officers of the court." Compulsively cruising Queen's Park on freezing nights, and bringing home outlandish men, was not the proper behavior for an officer of one of Her Majesty's courts of law.

I dropped out of law school at the end of the first year. By fall, I found myself in an ashram in Rishikesh, India (the Beatles went there a few years later), studying Yoga to learn how to master my sexual urges. Whatever else Yoga did for me, it did not diminish or stifle my libidinal force. I returned to Canada, this time to Montreal, but could not cope with the cold weather, and went to Mexico City to seek my fortune.

I arrived in Mexico on January 1, 1957. I fell in love with the country and its people instantly. The balmy climate, the scenery, the architecture, and the friendliness of the people endeared Mexico to me. It helped that I was enormously attracted to Mexican men. I liked the color of their skin, their facial features, and their habitual smiling.

Within two weeks I found a job, a place to live, and various cruising spots. I also started studying Spanish on my own, practicing my newly acquired vocabulary on everybody I met.

In Mexico City the large parks, the wide boulevards, and even the small *glorietas* (miniparks with a fountain in the center) were good cruising places. There was a lot of public sex going on in these places, but that was not my style.

In Toronto I had been tongue-tied when trying to make conversation with fellow cruisers. In Mexico City I boldly addressed whomever I liked, managing quite well with my very limited Spanish. There was a new vitality to my cruising. I did not just need to get it on because I was driven; I wanted to have sex with the beautiful and *simpático* guys who surrounded me.

I remember well my first encounter. I went cruising immediately after I had rented a modern, furnished studio apartment, and had secured a job for myself. I met Jaime early in the evening, on the Paseo de la Reforma, a wide, elegant boulevard in the center of the city. He was a fairly tall guy, about my own age, with dark brown hair and eyes. Even though he looked more like a southern European than a Latino I liked him immediately, because of his open and frank smile, and cheerful expression.

We went to my place and chatted for a long while. Being able to converse with him in Spanish gave me an intellectual high. Eventually, seductively, he pulled me toward the bed. In Toronto, sex had been somber and purposeful; lovemaking in Mexico City was cheerful and lighthearted. When I had sex in Toronto, I considered myself a wayward officer of the court. In Mexico I was just plain José, the new cruising persona I had assumed.

When we were done, Jaime addressed me solemnly. I did not understand everything he said. What came through clearly was that his father, mother, and elder brother were in terrible *apuros*. These *apuros*—tribulations—could be overcome with God's help, which was paramount, and, to a much lesser extent, with money. The lesser help, that of money, would be my contribution to solving the *apuros* of Jaime's family.

I was confused. I had read and heard that homosexuals were often subject to blackmail. I was certain that Jaime was not blackmailing me. Well, then, he was asking me to *pay* for sex. He was a male prostitute!

"How much do you . . . ," here I mentally replaced "want" with "need."

Jaime came up with a sum of money that was almost equivalent to the monthly rent for my studio. I looked blankly at him. He understood my expression. "How much can you help me with?" he asked.

I had not done all that well for myself in India with my Yoga studies. But to survive there, with very little money, I had learned some fancy haggling techniques. Now I put them to use. As an opening gambit, I offered Jaime one-twentieth of what he had asked for. Even this amount would almost have paid a day's wages of an ordinary employee. To my surprise, he was very happy with my first counteroffer. He assured me that it would go a long way to free his father, mother, and elder brother from their sundry *apuros*. I did not make another date with Jaime because I was disappointed that I had had to pay for sex, even though the money went for a good cause.

The second guy, whose name I have long forgotten, picked me up as soon as I sat on a bench at my neighborhood's *glorieta*. He was not as cute as Jaime but much darker, with sharp Aztec facial features that made him attractive to me. When we finished with sex, he addressed me with the same grave solemnity Jaime had employed two days earlier. His *apuros* were more limited. Only his mother was in the hospital but her situation was *muy grave*. Primarily, he beseeched the Almighty for help, as he always did in such situations, and, secondarily, he fervently hoped that I would offer some assistance as well. Could I help him with . . . and he asked for an amount smaller than what I had offered Jaime a few days earlier. To be fair, I gave him the same amount I had given Jaime.

The third person, Javier, I saw twice before he made his move. Javier studied English after school and we communicated quite well with each other. Javier's plan for me, which he disclosed at the end of the second session, was to underwrite his studies, seeing that I was five years older, wealthier, and also, according to him, wiser. I still had no desire to pay for sex. I did not take him up on his offer to sponsor his studies even though we had had a very good time. I gave him what I had given to the two other guys and dismissed him from my life.

Analyzing all this with the gift of hindsight, the three guys I saw in about ten days, and most of the many others I saw later on throughout Mexico, were opportunistic rather than professional hustlers. They were doing their cruising, and, if they met an enormously rich person like myself, they would ask him to help out with the various *apuros* of their families.[2]

That I was very rich became obvious to my companions once they were in my studio apartment. It was modern, had a kitchenette and bathroom, and was located in a good neighborhood. But, above all, I lived by myself. In those days (and even today) having the luxury of living alone made one unique. Years later, I rented a two-room flat in a fairly large building catering to the middle class. I was the *only* tenant who had that much private space. All other apartments were occupied by families with children.

Had I known how to get it, plenty of free sex was available. People in the know cruised specific straight bars where gays would meet. (There were no exclusively gay bars in those days.) The street cruisers were the least elegant members of the gay set.

Pretty soon it became clear to me that I would always have to pay for sex in Mexico. The sad stories of my partners would vary, but the bottom line would be the same.

Compared to Toronto, I was now in paradise. I picked up cute and *simpático* sex partners every single time I went cruising. I enjoyed the lighthearted sex and the chit-chat in Spanish, and did not experience neurotic anxieties. Many of my partners were not well educated. One was even illiterate. But I was improving my Spanish.

There was one problem in paradise. My role as the financial savior of my sexual partners was getting to be very expensive. In Toronto I had cruised, reluctantly and rarely, when I could not abide my sexual loneliness any longer. In Mexico City, I cruised often and joyfully, but it was costing me a pretty peso.

There was also a surcharge imposed by the infamous Mexican *mordida* system. Every so often, while cruising, I was stopped by a vice cop (more likely someone pretending to be a cop, though I did know that at the time) extorting a trivial amount of money. I took this in stride. After all, in Toronto I could have been arrested, tried, and jailed. In Mexico, I was squeezed sometimes for just walking and looking, but it could be taken care of with a small handout.

I worked as a full-time teacher at a private school and did a lot of tutoring on the side. By local standards, I was pretty well off financially, especially since I had only myself to support. I was free four or five evenings a week. I would have loved to cruise every one of these evenings, but I simply did not make enough money to indulge my whim.

I decided to draw up a budget for my sexual expenses. That meant that I had to know ahead of time how much I would spend on each encounter before bringing anyone home with me. Therefore, I would tell all my prospective companions how many pesos I could spend to help them with whatever tribulations they and their families faced.

This approach was decidedly un-Mexican. Their standard obligatory reply was always the same: "But I do not dedicate myself to that" (meaning prostitution). With a great deal of diplomacy, we would agree on a reasonable remuneration, after many assurances on my part that the money was a contribution toward their families' welfare, not a fee for sex.

It was quite a struggle for me stick to my budget. But it worked because it saved me from worrying that I was spending too much money on hustlers. I budgeted by the month. If my monthly budget was 300 pesos then, on the tenth of the month, only 100 pesos should have been used up. This way I knew that if I did not have the funds on a given evening, a few days hence there would be enough money in the kitty to go cruising.

It took a number of trips to Mexico before I understood fully the alpha and omega of Mexican homosexuality: *penetration.* In Mexico, penetration has a symbolic significance that transcends the physical aspect of the act itself. Apparently, because my partners expected me to pay for sex with them, they did not impose the Mexican sexual code on me. On my first trip to Mexico, I got away without screwing or being screwed, which, for a number of reasons, I did not want to do then. Merrily, I climaxed by dry humping my partners. (This practice is also known as frottage.)

My partners climaxed the same way, or allowed me to blow them. (In those days, they would never have blown me. They considered this practice a foreign barbarity. Many Mexicans still do.) It is absolutely inconceivable that, had I been Mexican, I would have been allowed to neither screw nor be screwed!

* * *

I had been working in Mexico illegally for five months. My papers could have been arranged but with a horrendous bribe. My legal status was precarious, compromising the school. I had to return to Toronto. I felt as Adam must have felt just before the expulsion from the Garden of Eden.

In Toronto I found a job as the special events coordinator at a community center. I imagined myself to be in the public eye, and felt that I needed to be very circumspect. My cruising anxieties returned. I was as unsuccessful as I had always been there. Whereas in Mexico I had always found partners whom I liked physically, in Toronto I again had to make do with men I did not care for particularly. I assume that many of these men did not care much for me either. The inevitable result was always just a better-than-nothing encounter.

Most of all, I resented the time I spent on unproductive cruising. I had a busy schedule at work. I continued my Spanish studies, took prerequisite courses for my master's degree, and held a part-time job. The long cruising sessions annoyed and frustrated me. Even then, I considered time a more precious commodity than money.

In Mexico, all my contacts turned out to be hustlers. In Toronto, I had never encountered one. I assumed that they hung out at certain locations but I did not know where these were.

I had lots of compensatory time off at work and used it twice a year for vacations in Mexico. With my newly acquired Spanish, I also traveled to Puerto Rico and Spain. In these places too I met hustlers easily.

This feast abroad and famine in Toronto went on for a number of years. Then I obtained a position in San Francisco, applied for a visa to the USA, and resigned from my job in Toronto. Now I felt myself free from the imaginary limelight that had engulfed me at work. Free at last, I asked a fellow cruiser at Queen's Park where one could meet hustlers. Disdainfully, he told me the location.

It was a street corner not far from Queen's Park. There, hustlers would congregate around the clock, though there was more choice at night. To my delight, ethnic minorities had some representatives on this corner. The third or fourth guy I met there became my "regular." His name was Albert. He was nineteen years old, skinny, and short. His blood was a cocktail of many ethnic groups, but the First Nation (Indian) predominated. He was very shy and also extremely passionate. I suspect he had a drinking problem, which he tried to hide.

As with my Mexican sex partners, I looked forward to seeing Albert: not to get off and get it over with, but to be with someone I *enjoyed* looking at and having sex with.

We saw each other every few days. Sometimes, he stood me up. Maybe he was drunk on these occasions. When that happened, I would go to the hustlers' corner and pick up someone else I liked. Albert and I always had a good time. I liked his shyness, and he was happy that someone was ready to listen to him and take him seriously. I had just acquired my first TV set. Albert stayed at my place until late in the evening watching programs he enjoyed, while I did my Spanish homework at the other end of the room. I took him out for dinner a few times. None of his other clients had done this.

Fraternizing with hustlers—above and beyond what is necessary for sex—is considered by many as a sign of loneliness. In retrospect, was it loneliness that prompted me to befriend Albert, in a limited fashion, in addition to having sex with him? For close to three years I had coordinated public events, from dance festivals to political forums, and was not the least bit starved for social intercourse. It was physical intimacy that I was sorely missing! I wanted to unite these intimacies—something I had never managed to achieve until meeting Albert.

I resigned my job at the community center expecting to leave for San Francisco within a few weeks. But the paperwork for my visa did not go through for half a year. Finally freed from my high-profile job, I could do as I pleased in Toronto. Now I allowed myself to cruise Queen's Park regularly. I even met sex partners fairly frequently. But because they were only *very* marginally my type, I was not particularly interested in their company after the mediocre sex session was over. They, too, after the lukewarm session, were not eager for my company.

With Albert it was different. We always had good sex, and, aesthetically, I enjoyed being in his company after we were done. Most of the time, he watched TV. While I was doing my own work, I was pleased that such an appealing guy was in the same room with me. For his part, my place was more cheerful than his own shared accommodations, and I did not argue with him about which program he could watch.

I liked Albert as a person, and was happy to add a social component to the sex act. I certainly did not buy his time. I did not have the wherewithal to do that. Albert must have had a pretty good idea of my financial circumstances. After all, I lived in a furnished studio apartment.

After seeing Albert regularly for a month or so, I fell in love madly with someone I had met socially. His name was Joel. He was a few years younger than I, and, to my surprise, of fair complexion. As a matter of fact, he could have passed for my younger brother. Joel was a music student—an aspiring violinist.

For some three weeks we saw each other as often as possible. It wasn't only that we had good sex. We went out of town together for a weekend, and took in two concerts and a few movies. Joel spent so much time at my place that I assumed he would move in with me. I started toying with the idea of giving up on moving to San Francisco.

A few days into this affair, Albert called me for a date. I had all but forgotten about him. I informed him that I was dating someone and that his services would no longer be required. I almost told him, "See, I can get it on, for *free*, with a guy I like even better than you."

It was just as well that I had not told Albert that. From the very beginning, Joel behaved strangely, as if he had mental problems. I chose to ignore it. One evening Joel came by and, in a very agitated frame of mind, told me, "I am seeing the world from the wrong end of the telescope. We have to stop doing what we have been doing!"

"But what's wrong, Joel?"

"I haven't told you. I am a patient at the Toronto Forensic Clinic. My therapist would have a fit if he knew that we are having sex!"

"What is the Forensic Clinic?"

"It is a clinic for sex offenders who go there by court order. But they also take voluntary patients with sexual disorders."

"What is *your* disorder?"

"The same as yours. We are homosexuals. My therapist says that we are all really sociopaths." A few minutes later, Joel was out of my house and my life.

I was heartbroken. Now some of Joel's oddities made sense to me. For instance, he had not given me his address or phone number. I had no way of getting in touch with him. But I did not really understand what had happened—how overnight, without apparent reason, our affair ended so abruptly. The Joel incident was the harbinger of the many misadventures I would experience in my nonhustler relationships, including therapists alienating my companions, constant kaleidoscopic affairs and, above all, inexplicably odd behavior by my partners.

Eventually, I sought out Albert and resumed our paid-for relationship. I could have afforded to see Albert more often, but I forced myself to spend one evening a week cruising. I did not want to have to pay for sex always.

Sex for money was an easier proposition in Mexico. There was no question in my mind that in Mexico I was economically much better situated than all of my partners. Not only were they poor, but they really had to help support their huge families. It was a charitable act to help them out.

In Toronto, when I still had my job, I drew an average salary, commensurate with my position. Albert, just like me, could have found a job and supported himself. I was still brainwashed by the social mores that condemned paying for sex, especially if both parties enjoyed the experience. It took me many years to formulate correctly the question I should have asked myself in Toronto: "Am I satisfied with Albert's services?" rather than "What is Albert's justification for hustling?"

At that time, the first exclusively gay bathhouse opened in Toronto. It was called The Roman Baths. I would go there once a week, and usually hate every moment of it. Nobody I liked wanted to have anything to do with me. As always, the few men who desired me did not interest me at all. Now that I saw Albert and other hustlers, searching for free sex made even less sense to me.

* * *

I took to San Francisco right away. Ever so slowly, I started coming out of the closet, and for the first time in my life had gay friends. I was also much more successful sexually in this city than I had been in Toronto. I found more ethnic variety here, and was more attractive to other gays. But I still preferred the ease of meeting hustlers.

When I arrived in San Francisco at the end of 1964, it was still safe to cruise at Union Square. In the evenings, time permitting, I would go to the park and cruise for a while. Then, if I had not found a suitable partner, I would go across the street, where Geary intersects Powell, at the south side of the St. Francis Hotel. The better-class hustlers would hang out there, to the great chagrin of the hotel's management. (The corner of Market and Mason Streets was reserved for the less classy hustlers.) I would find a suitable hustler and take him home. My goal was to end each of my cruising sessions with a companion in tow—free if possible, paid for if necessary!

After a few weeks I had a small pool of favorite hustlers to choose from. The hustlers and I became friendly with each other. As I had learned to do in Mexico, I made up a sex budget and stuck to it.

Without the constraints of a budget, I probably would have dispensed with cruising altogether and picked up only hustlers. These hustlers were usually more physically appealing, and often socially even more enjoyable than the people I met at the square.

My Union Square days were numbered. Within two years it became too dangerous to cruise the square. Hippies started dealing drugs there, attracting hoods and unwanted police attention. Going to bars on a regular basis was not my thing. Alcohol has always made me groggy and cranky rather than merry, and I could not stand the loud music and the smoke. I started doing my cruising at the many gay bathhouses that used to exist in San Francisco. Unfortunately, it was logistically and financially impossible to exercise the Union Square option of seeing a hustler the same evening if things did not work out in the bathhouse. Once again, I was involved in lengthy and frequently frustrating cruising.

At the San Francisco baths I made out better than in Toronto because there were more men I liked in them and, mysteriously, I myself had become more popular. (Maybe my bathhouse-cruising techniques had improved.) But the results were *always* unpredictable. Too often, after many hours, I would return home without scoring.

On a rare good night, I would have sex with several guys I liked. As a point of fact, I met my first lover at a bathhouse.

What disturbed me most—and still does—was the emotional roller coaster of gay life. The sexual partners at the baths, with whom I had had such passionate sex, and with whom I had exchanged phone numbers, would often show no interest in future meetings when I called them afterward. Sometimes even the phone numbers they gave me were phony.

Of course, not all of my experiences with hustlers were without problems. But there was a difference between hustler problems and potential-boyfriend disappointments. The former could be replaced with newer and better versions. The latter—like the flakes at the baths with their phony telephone numbers—were not so easily dismissed. For a very long time, I blamed myself for failing to get to the dating stage with the passionate lovers I kept meeting at the baths. It was difficult for me to understand how the guys I had such passionate sex with at the baths would lose all interest in me as soon as they encountered the next trick.

Until the San Francisco baths closed in the early 1980s, due to the AIDS crisis, I would visit them about once a week, to prove to myself that I could get it for free. Of course, it was not entirely free. Admission to the baths, with a private room, was fairly costly.

I had learned to apply different standards to bathhouse patrons than to hustlers. A youthful and cute (not necessarily handsome) face, with a decent body and, ideally, a cheerful personality, was what I required of my hustlers. At the baths, I kept lowering these standards as the night grew longer, the search more tedious, and the rejections more numerous. The result was that the "free" bathhouse sexual partners were, frequently, not the least bit my type.

Eventually, the street-hustling scene became too dangerous for me.[3] I stopped picking up street hustlers and started choosing them through ads in gay publications. Once I liked a particular hustler, I would work out a financial arrangement, and see him regularly. (One hustler I saw, off and on, over a period of ten years.)

To this day, I still do my "duty." I try to connect with partners who do not charge. These days I do it through personal ads in gay and semi-gay publications. I have had my share of luck in these endeavors—though free is not always really free—but I am still *much* happier with the predictability and physical appearance of hustlers.

In retrospect, I feel good about the many thousand dollars I have spent on hustlers. I have derived a great deal of pleasure from being with them. I do regret the countless hours I have wasted cruising the parks and baths in Toronto, San Francisco, and elsewhere.

Gay life is not all about sex. I have made a lot of very close nonsexual gay friends in many countries, and these friendships have enhanced my life tremendously. However, sex is inextricably intertwined with being homosexual. Had it not been for hustlers, my gay life would have been an incessant whine about not having enough good sex. I know many gays, young and old, handsome and homely, who feel shortchanged at the bars, baths, and clubs. Thanks to hustlers, I have done very well for myself in my sexual pursuits. I salute the many hustlers who have helped make my gay existence a joyful one.

* * *

Before I close this chapter, I want to explain how I have come to know so much about hustlers. Many gay men avail themselves of hustlers but they keep this to themselves. Some older gay men were themselves hustlers in their younger days, but it is their big secret. Because I have been very open about my own experiences with hustlers, quite a few former hustlers have told me about their pasts. Friends and acquaintances who avail themselves of hustlers clandestinely have confided in me as well. Thus, for example, I know a fair amount about bodybuilders who are hustlers, as well as about their clients, though I myself have never been intimate with one.

Late in life, I have taken up writing gay-travel guidebooks. This has given me insight I would not have gleaned from personal experience. For instance, in my capacity as a writer, I was allowed with my camera into the dormitory of a group of transvestite hustlers in San José, Costa Rica. I would never have picked up any of them, nor, had I been their client, would they have answered my very personal questions. I feel privileged that they shared with me very intimate information and permitted me to tell their stories.[4]

* * *

A few months ago I received a phone call from a man who had read my Mexico guidebook. He told me that he was grateful for the information about the puzzling hustler scene in that country. "Your book explained to me," he said, "why guys always asked me for handouts and gifts. This used to bother me a lot. Thanks to your book I now understand how the system works. On my last trip, I made friends with a man I met in Acapulco. He says he is straight, but we have good sex together. He expects me to help him with his endless series of crises. I don't care. I have the money and I am out there to enjoy myself, not to prove a point."

"Prove what point?" I asked.

"That I can get it for free. Sure, there's free sex at most steam baths in Mexico. But they are really dirty places. And, in any case, I want to get it on with guys who turn me on, not with some ugly man I happen to meet at the baths. I never cared about the money. As a matter of principle I did not want to pay. Now I know better."

I am happy that I have helped change at least one man's perception about obtaining good sex.

Chapter 2

The Hustler
As an Independent Contractor

I planned on spending a few hours reading the hustler ads in a number of gay publications, and then selecting a few of them to make a point. It turns out that the first two columns of "model" ads (model is a euphemism for hustler), in the first gay publication, supplied all the information I needed.

Here are seven samples, from a local gay publication, listed under Models/Escorts (names and phone numbers deleted):[1]

1. **Extremely Handsome College Student**
Masculine, clean cut & yes versatile
French/Italian, thick dk, full lips
Very hot! Hung & tight. Out only

2. **Oral Slave**
Hot Mouth, Deep Throat
Gdlooking, 5'11", 155#, 36, $75
Available Wknites & Wkends

3. **Affectionate Warm**
Youthful 5'8", 140 lbs, clean cut
Smooth. For a hot session call me

4. **Piss On You**
Nasty Italian Top $125

5. **Slaves Trained**
38 yo 6'1", 210# porn magazine model
Call Master . . .

6. To Serve Or Be Served?
What Is Your Pleasure
Hungry, Affectionate, 22, out

7. Hot Masculine Guy, 30 Big Bone
KICKS BACK FOR ORAL SERVICE
$60 IN Days OK

These ads are enough to destroy all stereotypes regarding hustlers. If you have thought of hustlers as run-of-the-mill sex workers, be forewarned: each one has a unique style. For instance, if you confuse the phone number of worker 3 with that of number 4, you will literally be pissed on instead of cuddled!

A common stereotype is that hustlers are young guys. Hustlers 2, 5, and 7 state in their ads that they are in their thirties. It is a safe bet that one or two of the other advertisers are in the same age bracket. Very recently, a new trend started, at least in San Francisco—*old* hustlers advertising their services, at a slight discount. For instance:

Naked Runner, 51 yo $40[2]

This ad is significant for another reason. There are those who justify hustlers' high fees because youth is fleeting and sex workers can practice their trade for only a few years. The Runner, as well as advertisers 2, 5, and 7 belie this theory.

So you think hustlers sell love for money? Hustlers 4 and 5 sell kinky fantasies. Number 4 makes quite sure that prospective clients do not mistake his sessions for lovemaking. He bills himself as a "nasty top," and charges his clients more than the others for the honor of being pissed on. Most likely, he makes out as well, or better, than the others.

Hustler 7 is in a category all by himself. Graciously, he will allow clients to suck on his "big bone." He probably realizes that his repertoire is quite limited, so he offers two incentives: a low economy price, and convenient hours. Hustler 2 is the flip side of 7. He, too, is somewhat limited. Like 7, who loves to be blown, 2 wants to be paid for fulfilling *his* fantasy of being an "oral slave."

Only numbers 1 and 6 come close to being all-around hustlers, who are there to please their clients by fulfilling the latter's sexual needs. As a matter of fact, only number 1 comes close to a preconceived notion of what hustlers are all about: he is a good-looking, young, and versatile college student. At least, this is what his ad claims.

What do these advertisers have in common? They are not down-and-out indigent folks. All of them have phones and pagers, and enough money to pay for the ads. Five of them have private living spaces that are decent enough for hosting their clients.

None of them follows a script. They work when it is convenient for them, sell a take-it-or-leave-it service package, and put a monetary value on their services that makes sense only to themselves. (Why would number 4—the pisser—ask for $125, almost the top fee for all hustlers in this publication?) They are truly independent contractors, carving out their particular niches in the market.

There are, of course, many hustlers who do not work from their homes, or do out calls (going to clients' homes).[3] They hang out in certain streets and bars. Later in this work, I describe the difference between "models," masseurs, and street hustlers. For now, let me point out that street hustlers, who lack the luxury of specifying their specialties in the media, are much more likely to be "generalists," that is, all around practitioners of gay sex. Even so, they, too, set limits on what acts they will or will not do, on a take-it-or-leave-it basis. Some, for instance, will tell their clients that they get screwed only by their lovers, others that they do not French kiss. Most, not all, German hustlers will offer a blow job as a matter of course, while most of their Mexican counterparts will reject this act out of hand.[4]

In many ways, street hustlers are even more independent than models. They observe no time frame, adhere to no schedule, make appointments reluctantly, and rarely keep them. They can walk away from clients they dislike. Doing so is a much stickier scenario for models, both with in and out calls.

Because hustlers are often regarded as the counterpart of female prostitutes, it is vital to understand the independent-contractor nature of hustling. Female prostitution brings a lot of heavy baggage with it: vicious pimps; strong males beating up weaker females; venereal diseases; and the tremendous difficulties facing "fallen women" who want to liberate themselves from this trade.

This kind of baggage has little or nothing to do with the male hustler. He has no pimps to answer to, is physically as strong as—often stronger than—his client, is as likely or unlikely to spread venereal diseases as any other casual gay-sex partner (a subject I'll discuss at length later), and can weave in and out of the hustling scene relatively easily.[5]

Female prostitution, by definition, involves an active male penetrating a passive female. I am sure there are many refinements and innovations that a good female prostitute can add to this scenario. However, there is no likelihood that the roles would be reversed, that is, the prostitute penetrating her clients. When a man hires a hustler, who will penetrate whom is an issue that needs to be worked out between the parties!

The sample ads illustrate not only the variety of services offered by hustlers but also that the hustlers who will not penetrate or be penetrated have different tricks in their repertoire which are good enough to please their clients.

* * *

In a recent ABC *20/20* TV program[6] exploring prostitution in the 1990s, a heterosexual interviewee states, "Of course I would like to get sex for free. But women are not interested in me." For gays the situation is somewhat different.

When I used to go to the baths there was always *someone* I could have gotten it on with (for free). The problem was not finding a sex partner but, rather, finding an acceptable one. Sometimes, in the wee hours of the morning, just to get it over with to catch some sleep before going to work, I did it with someone I was not attracted to at all. Later, I would hate myself for having done it.[7]

The availability issue is where the hustler's main role comes into play: he ensures the quality of the encounter in a convenient time frame. Unlike the female prostitute, who provides sex that might otherwise be unavailable at all to her heterosexual partner, the hustler provides quality sex to his client, compared to just getting off.

I have been told more than once that I do not appreciate the chase. It would be more accurate to say that I do not appreciate the hunt without the trophy. I have no quarrel with gays who, unlike me, enjoy the chase and do not care whether they score or not. But there are many people I know who constantly hunt unsuccessfully, and then complain bitterly how unfulfilled they are sexually. They are the ones who would benefit from the services of hustlers. What deters them is that they buy into the heterosexual self-loathing for using what they consider the male equivalent of a female prostitute.

Female prostitution is regarded by the world at large as an exploitative practice. Hustling is tarred with the same brush. Unfortunately, many hustlers, as well as their clients, buy into this viewpoint. Expressions like "exploitative sex" are bandied around—though it is far from clear who is exploiting whom. Clients who sense that the hustler is having as good a time as they are *and* is being paid for it sometimes feel exploited by the arrangement. Hustlers, when they have to put up, in their lingo, with assholes, sometimes feel that no amount of money can compensate them. (Members of other professions do not have to put up with assholes?) The good thing about hustling, compared to female prostitution controlled by pimps, is that either party can terminate an unsatisfactory relationship at will.

A corollary view maintains that hustling damages the practitioner physically and emotionally. I have had the opportunity to observe a number of hustlers over long periods of time. Many years of hustling have not healed the ones who were damaged, nor damaged the ones who were whole.

More to the point, really, is that lots of jobs involve a certain amount of danger. For instance, I have been reading a lot lately about the meatpacking industry. Meatpackers' pay has gone down to just above minimum wage. Workers in this industry are almost certain to experience episodes of carpal tunnel syndrome, and serious injuries to their hands are a reasonable expectation.

Models operating out of their homes probably have a *less* stressful existence than many other workers. (Of course, they do experience some stress, especially on the first date with a client.) Their unique advantage is that most of their clients, *certainly* not all, understand that if they want hustlers to show them a good time, they need to be nice to them. In the real world, bosses and supervisors often go out of their way to be nasty to their subordinates. Also, like any other independent contractor, a hustler is free to discontinue his working relationship with a client he does not like. Most people in the work place have to put up with the same untenable situations for years on end![8]

Some hustlers buy into society's view that hustling is degrading.[9] Ironically, it is the degradation imputed to hustling that senselessly drives up the fees of the practitioners. Hustlers do not earn as much as one would think when reading their ads. This point will be discussed at length later on. But they do get a spectacular amount of money for relatively easy and fast work. Just look at sample 4!

I know personally one of the advertisers in the above sample. He is a part-time hustler. Recently, he was very proud when he obtained a data-input job at $12 per hour, a $4 raise from his previous work. The job involves a one-hour commute each way, with a schedule that ruins both his days and evenings, and robs him of his weekends. As a hustler he works out of his home, is picked up by his clients, or is given cab fare. He charges somewhere between $75 and $100 for about an hour of his time. Often clients add a tip.

A fair and *very* generous compensation for his services, based on what he can he earn at a regular job, would be $25. Throw in another $5 to cover his ad and phone expense, and make it $30. He would be delighted to make that much money at any part-time job, except when working as a hustler. The markup is a compensation for the imputed degradation of male prostitution, to make it "worth his while." Miraculously, at $100 per session, the "degradation" of prostitution becomes a yuppie "modeling" or "escorting" job.[10]

Chapter 3

Hustling—A Vocation?

In the late 1970s, an enterprising San Franciscan came up with a neat idea. He would go through the hustlers' ads in the gay papers, make anonymous dates with the advertisers, and rate their services by awarding them stars. He called his publication *David's World*. For a while, some San Francisco hustler ads would state: "* * * in *David's World.*" Few ads displayed four stars—the highest possible ranking. And, needless to say, no hustler advertised a low ranking in *David's World*. Most displayed three stars.

Alfonso, a model, told me about the rating method, after he himself had gone through the interview. To attain a four-star rating a hustler had to be reasonably attractive, well-groomed, have a pleasant personality, and live in a presentable environment. He also had to be able to perform adequately the following tasks: make good body contact, be willing to screw and be screwed, blow, and French kiss. Alfonso, who did not get screwed by clients, earned three stars.

I relate this story to make the point that hustling is not a passive activity, in which the client does all the work, hands over money, and departs.

It is not even that simple when, one would assume, this is all the action the script dictates. For instance: a hustler, in drag, will be picked up by a "straight" client who, presumably, wants to have sex with a man while fantasizing that he is screwing a woman. What the client *really* wants is to be screwed by the female impersonator. This sort of thing happens even more frequently in Latin American countries where machismo is the name of the game.[1]

Because hustling is not merely a passive activity, the hustler needs to provide much more than just a receptive ass. To screw, he needs to have an erection. Some customers will insist that the hustler jack himself off and ejaculate while they are watching him. Others will insist that he go down on them. These activities may have to be performed even when the hustler is not the least bit attracted to his client.

For a hustler to be even moderately successful, having a pretty face and muscular body is neither necessary nor sufficient to guarantee success. Every time a hustler has sex with a new client he is confronted with a novel physical and psychological challenge. In spite of what society at large thinks about male prostitution, and how hustlers themselves might regard it, hustling is not just a job to make ends meet, but, rather, a vocation for which one must have a calling. By "calling" I mean natural skill and intuition, and the ability to learn from experience.

Of course hustling is about money—but there is a lot more to it. In the next chapter I will discuss the various reasons why a young (and quite often not-so-young) man chooses to become a hustler. While the reasons are complex and even convoluted the calling always needs to be there.

To illustrate my point, and put a human face on this theory, I will tell the story of my six-year affair with one hustler.

MAESTRO JED'S STORY

I met Jed in the summer of 1979 when hustlers still stood at the back of the St. Francis Hotel at Geary and Powell in San Francisco. Jed was twenty-three years old, slender, and of medium height. He had large green eyes, with long eyelashes, jet-black hair, and a remarkably large Adam's apple. I have heard it said that men with large Adam's apples are well-endowed, and that Jed certainly was. He was also one of those lucky guys who have an athletic build without having to work for it—broad-shouldered, with a slender waist, and a tight abdomen. Jed's skin was a bit on the tan side. He was the son of a German woman and a Hispanic man from New Mexico. Jed's father was probably a mixture of Native American, Mexican, and Spanish. Jed's facial features were a blend of his European lineage, and what Mexicans call *La Raza*—the ethnic blend of the New World.

I have shown Jed's (clothed) photos to many people. They almost always refer to him as "very sexy" and then invariably ask, "Is he well hung?" Nobody ever calls him handsome.

My first time with Jed was awkward. In the car he spoke little and did not make much sense. For such an indecisive person, he had a surprisingly assertive baritone voice. But he spoke very little. By the time we got home I thought of him as somewhat "slow," which made me feel better than classifying him as retarded.

As soon as we hit the bed I forgot all about his "slowness." Jed and I had already agreed on what type of sex we would have. But it is more fun if both parties enjoy the session. I asked Jed, "What do you like to do?" to which he replied, "I like to please."

Jed was versatile (by choice, I suspect, more bottom than top), knew intuitively how to turn me on, and seemed immensely pleased by whatever I did to him. It gave me the impression that the way we had sex was exactly what he had always wanted to do. He came abundantly just a few seconds before I climaxed. If he faked his own enjoyment, he was a very great actor!

In view of his brilliant bedroom performance I was willing to overlook his social ineptness. I asked him whether he would like to see me again but he was so uncommunicative that I gave up on him.

A few months later, I was at the Liberty baths. It was one of those nights when all the planets were aligned in the wrong positions. I was shunned and despised by everyone. Whomever I tried to approach fled in horror. Then I saw Jed.

He remembered me, and greeted me in a friendly manner. Naturally, I asked Jed whether he would come to my cubicle. "Maybe later," he said. "Or, maybe not. I am not having fun. I have been here for a long time. I might just leave."

I knew that on that particular night I would not score at the steam bath. I could hardly afford the expense of the admission to the bathhouse plus Jed's fee, but I justified it by telling myself that it would be good for my mental health. I asked Jed, "Why don't we leave together and go to my place? We'll work out the finances later."

"OK, if you want to," he said without much enthusiasm.

When we reached my home Jed asked, "Do you have any drugs?"

"No."

"Not even some pot?"

"No, Jed. I don't do drugs at all."

He seemed disappointed. However, now that he knew my sexual likes and dislikes, he surpassed his previous performance. I was sure that he had had some fun previously at the bath because he was completely spent after he climaxed. "You tired me out," he complained.

He saw a large package on the living room floor. "What's this?" he asked.

I had bought a folding door for the kitchen a few days earlier. "I'm looking for a handyman to install this door."

"I am a handyman."

"You are? This is what you do for a living?"

"No, I am a singer. But I know how to fix stuff."

"Where do you sing?"

"I do gigs here and there."

"Have you had any training?"

"Oh, I had a scholarship as a child at the San Francisco Conservatory of Music."

I had doubts about Jed's singing or mechanical abilities. He still seemed "slow" to me, at least out of bed. On the other hand, I wanted to get to know him better.

We agreed on a fee for his work and he promised to come by on Saturday, at 9 a.m. sharp, to install the door. He arrived at about eleven in the morning. To my surprise, he carried a toolbox.

Rapidly, without any fuss, he installed the door. I was impressed.

"How about us meeting on Monday night?" I asked.

"What for?"

"For sex."

"I don't like to make appointments. I'll give you my telephone number. Call me sometime."

It took two weeks for me to get hold of Jed. On two consecutive days, I spoke to two roommates who promised to give Jed my messages. On the third day, a mysterious woman answered and assured me that no Jed lived at that number. Then the telephone was "temporarily disconnected," probably for not paying the bill. When I finally reached Jed we made an appointment for that evening. He would meet me at Castro and 18th Street, at the bus stop, at 7 p.m. "sharp."

Those were the good days in San Francisco. Nowadays, you get a $250 ticket for just *thinking* abut parking in a bus zone. Then, one could get away with it. Still, I felt uncomfortable waiting for Jed well over twenty minutes right in the bus zone. When I scolded him for being late, he dismissed my reproof by saying, "I had to get a bite to eat. I have not eaten all day long. I showed up, didn't I?"

At home he asked me once again for drugs. Again, I told him that I did not do drugs. It took quite a few meetings before Jed believed that I did not do any drugs. Once, probably to test me, he brought some cocaine and offered to share it with me. "No, Jed, I really don't do drugs and I prefer not having them at my house."

"You're not much fun," he commented.

After a few sexual encounters, I was certain that if I saw Jed every few days for the rest of my life, I would not want or need any additional sex partners. Had Jed asked me to become monogamous with him I would have gladly agreed. Since I had become a "regular" we worked out a low fee of $25 per session. Nevertheless, always paying for sex would have amounted to a lot of money.

I did not need to worry. I never saw Jed in any pattern. He would move without giving me a new phone number, or do a gig out of town, or forget to show up when we made a date. I overlooked all of this because our sexual sessions were so intense.

All told, I had sex with Jed close to 200 times. Our sexual encounters ranged from very good to excellent. In spite of Jed's moodiness and his apparent disinterest in me as a person, not once did he falter in his performance. I am big on affection and kissing, and I got this in great abundance from Jed. He never made me feel that I was imposing on him sexually; but almost always he conveyed to me that I made unreasonable demands upon his time. Making appointments was a burden to him. The way he wanted things done was to call me when it suited his mood and needs. I would have to drive to his place, wait until he got ready, bring him to my home, and return him to base when we were done.

Jed did some New Wave gigs out of town and sometimes even got paid well. I know this to be true because I saw some of the programs, and helped him cash his checks. Apparently, he had some connections in the music field. But nothing permanent ever came of it.

He treated hustling like all his other temporary jobs. He had them for a while, lost them for not showing up, then tried something else. Once, he told me that he would place an ad in the paper and hustle out of his home. I felt threatened by it. Jed would have been entitled to charge a small fortune for each encounter, and would not need to bother with clients like me who were on a tight budget. I did not need to worry. Even if he had gotten around to writing the ad, paying to run it, acquiring an answering machine, and waiting for calls, Jed would not have kept his appointments with his clients. The reason that we saw so much of each other was due to my persistence. I never got tired of having sex with Jed, and grudgingly put up with his flakiness.

Over the years, we had our emotional ups and downs, though the sexual chemistry between us never changed. (The worse Jed's mood, the better was his sexual performance!) We were often displeased with each other: I, because Jed would be late or stand me up, or just be morose and in a bad mood; Jed, because I would fuss over inconsequential matters like being stood up. From time to time, he would borrow money from me, and was upset because I wanted to pin him down regarding an exact day and time for our next date.

But we also had good times. One summer we went to Guerneville, on the Russian River. We stayed at the Willows, a gay, rustic hotel overlooking the river. We spent most of the day on the river and I taught Jed to paddle and steer the canoe. At long last, Jed discovered that I had a useful skill I could impart to him. As soon as we changed and went out for dinner, guys started hitting on Jed. We had already decided beforehand that we would have sex after we ate and then Jed would go about town. "I can always score drugs in Guerneville. Dudes just offer them to me," he assured me.

Sex was wonderful that evening. I was content with our sexual session, and with not needing to fend off Jed's many suitors. He went out just before eleven. A few minutes later it started raining very heavily, the last thing one expects at the Russian River in August. I had not let Jed use my car. He knew how to drive, but, naturally, did not have a valid license. Even if he had a valid license, I would not have allowed him to use my car because of his drug activities.

Jed came back to the hotel. He was dripping water on the floor. "Let's go to the hot tub. I feel chilled," he said.

Other guests had the same idea. It was crowded in and around the tub. Lots of guys made passes at Jed. Once we returned to the room Jed grabbed me and threw me on the bed. We had sex for the second time that evening, and it was even better than the first time.

Jed never discussed his sexual tastes with me. I suspect that his on-and-off roommate was, at least for a while, his lover. The roommate, an unemployed graphic artist, lived on disability income. He was a plain-looking man a few years older than Jed. He had seen me often enough when I came by to pick Jed up, and was always friendly to me. Jed never told me anything about lovers, clients, or tricks. I knew that, from time to time, when he was short on funds, he would hustle.

Jed knew that I was unconditionally opposed to drugs. He never bothered to discuss, in depth, his drug habit. I do not know whether Jed did drugs so heavily because he had mental problems, or whether he had mental problems because of all the drugs he took.[2]

* * *

In the winter of 1985 Jed called me to arrange a time to install a new faucet in my kitchen. I had all but forgotten that he had promised to do this a few months earlier.

When he finished the work he said, "I am giving up hustling."

"Why?"

"I am seeing a psychotherapist now. She says that being a sex object is fucking with my mind."

I was shocked. "But, Jed, you are not a sex object!"

"What am I then?"

"A great sex maestro."

I could tell he was pleased with my spontaneous reply. I wondered then how he had found the resources to see a therapist. Maybe, I thought, pushing thirty was driving him to make changes in his life.

"I wish you a happy retirement, Jed," I said, "but I will miss you very much."

I felt very saddened to lose Jed. I did not believe that hustling was why Jed was so mixed up. But once the therapist told him this he would have made this association whenever we had sex. It would not have worked for either of us.

As uncommunicative as ever, Jed had no parting words for me.

* * *

I did not see or hear from him for two years. Then I ran into him in the street. He looked gaunt and his face was pinched. Still, to me he was just as attractive as he had always been. In answer to my question he said, "I am going to school now. I am taking up graphic design."

Years earlier Jed had shown me some of his drawings. I liked them. There seemed no reason why he would not make a good graphic designer.

I wondered whether Jed had AIDS. This would explain his seeing a therapist and his ability to go to school. He was probably receiving SSI. I was not worried about myself. I had been tested a few months earlier for the first time and was negative. Jed and I had had sex before we knew about AIDS. But whatever we did, first unsafely and later on taking precautions, Jed had never penetrated me. Not having been penetrated by anybody is the only explanation I have about why I have survived while so many others, who led the same lifestyle, perished.

It took yet another year for me to bump into Jed again. By then it was obvious that he had AIDS. We chatted for a while. "Call me sometime, Jed," I said as we parted.

"I may surprise you one of these days," he said.

A while later, I found out that a new acquaintance knew Jed well. "You know, don't you, that Jed is very sick," said the acquaintance. "He'll probably die soon."

"No, I did not know that. Please give him my regards. I would like to visit him. Would you find out whether he would want to see me?"

A few days later my new acquaintance called to tell me that Jed had passed away. He had, however, received my regards before he died. I was given instructions about a memorial service for him. In death, as during his entire life, something went wrong. The address was not quite right and I could not find the place.

* * *

In retrospect, Jed and I had an arrangement that enriched both of us. I feel privileged that for some six years I had incredibly fulfilling sexual experiences with a great sex maestro.

In spite of what Jed's psychologist told him, our arrangement was good for him. On a number of occasions, I saved Jed from becoming homeless by lending him rent money. Many times I allowed him to use my phone number when applying for a job. I provided him with a decent income in return for pleasant work. (I'll state it again: I do not believe he could have faked his pleasure when having sex with me over such a long period!) I did not "buy" Jed. By paying him, I acquired slivers of Jed's time *when* I needed it.

Rest in peace, Jed. I shall always remember our lovemaking. Yes, of course, paid lovemaking. So what?

* * *

In and of itself, having a vocation for hustling does not make much change for a potential hustler. Jed also had a vocation for singing and very little came of it. As in any other profession, a variety of skills and a lot of discipline are essential to make a go of it. But, for hustlers without the calling, things are different: they wash out early or become petty or serious criminals.

Even without the social prejudice against hustling, it is a complicated job. Without the vocation, it can become an odious one for the practitioner. Those who stick with it, without having a vocation, often find illegitimate ways to make it a happier field of endeavor. I will discuss this in the chapter about safety.

Sometimes, when the hustler has an especially strong vocation for the profession, the interaction between him and his client can be a source of great psychological as well as physical delight. I will close with an anecdote about encounters with such a hustler.

OSCAR'S STORY

I have always taken great pride in the fact that I climax when I am ready to do so. More often than not, I manage to pace myself, and come simultaneously with my partner. My encounters with Oscar were very different.

In the 1960s, Oscar was a part-time hustler standing at the St. Francis Hotel waiting to be picked up. He was a Chicano guy, in his early twenties, cute rather than handsome. He always had a ready smile for a prospective client, and a real gift for gab. He held a job of some sort, and managed to rent a decent studio apartment close to the St. Francis Hotel. He took his clients there, making good use of his time.

There is a tacit, conventional understanding between hustlers and clients that, once the client climaxes, the scene is officially over. The first time I was with Oscar, I was out of his place in less than twenty minutes. This had never happened to me before!

On that occasion, Oscar had not rushed me at all. After a few minutes together in bed, Oscar deciphered the code to my orgasm preference. Without discussing it, and while displaying great affection, he maneuvered himself into the ideal frottage-bottom position. Then, moving his body synchronously with mine, as in a precisely choreographed dance, he *made* me come!

The second time around I took up the challenge. Without talking to him about his technique, I decided to resist it. I was not going to climax until I was good and ready, and I would drag it out as much as possible. By sheer willpower, I lasted some five minutes longer than the previous time. Oscar understood my sexuality better than I did myself and, once again, *made* me climax.

A few weeks later I ran into him in the street. "Hey, Joseph," he said, "let's go to my place and have some fun."

This was before the advent of the ATM. "I don't have enough money on me," I said.

"Don't worry about it. I'll give you credit."

In the world of street hustlers, I had just been awarded a medal. Oscar did not even know where I lived, had he wanted to collect the money in person. I was very flattered. "I'll be happy to turn a trick with you, Oscar. But, please, don't make me come so fast."

Oscar looked at me wistfully for a moment, and then grinned broadly. "So you know my secret. OK, I won't make you come."

"What do you mean, 'secret?' Isn't it obvious to your other clients?"

"Not to most of them."

"How come?"

"They think they are just super horny when they are with me, and that's why they come so fast."

We went to his place. Some twenty minutes into the action he asked, "Are you ready now?"

"Give me a few more minutes."

After a while he asked, "Now?"

"OK." A minute later, he *made* me climax. We made a date for the following week. On that occasion, I gave him the money for both sessions.

There have been two other hustlers in my life who could make me climax when they willed it. I knew, and they knew, that they had the *power.* My body was the instrument on which they played their sexual rhapsody. When the hustler has a vocation, the sexual encounter becomes magical for the client. One hopes that the hustler enjoys it as well.

Chapter 4

Why Hustlers Hustle

SPECTACULAR BUT INADEQUATE PAY

Full-time street hustlers do not, as a rule, make much money, although it would seem that they are compensated spectacularly for turning a trick. A street hustler who could earn a *maximum* of $8 per hour (minus deductions) working for a retailer will net $80 for spending an hour or less with a client. Therefor, he will sincerely believe that he is paid handsomely per hour. If he factored in the time he spends, in all sorts of bad weather, waiting for clients, he would realize that he really earns minimum wage for hard and dangerous work. Such insight would force him to admit to himself that full-time hustling is no more lucrative than many other menial jobs he could perform. This is a message that he is loath to hear.

It is not only the hours they have to put in. The waiting itself can become an extremely dangerous occupation: being attacked by other hustlers or busted by the police are distinct possibilities. How much they earn is, at the end of the day, of little practical importance. Much of it is often spent on drugs, alcohol, and useless trinkets, because this is part of the lifestyle on the street.

A new face on the street will attract many buyers. A novice hustler may make a tidy fortune during his first weeks on the job. Forever after, he will remember his $500 first day and disdain a regular job where, after deductions, he would earn one-tenth of this amount.

Hustlers working out of their homes can earn a decent wage, even after deducting their overhead for ads and pager service. However, to do this they have to be willing to answer the phone at all hours, contend with nuisance calls, and have sex after the bars close. For the lucrative out calls, they really need their own transportation. It is not an easy way of making a living, though it circumvents the discipline of the workplace.

There are, however, two classes of hustlers who do well for themselves: the part-timers and the specialists. Part-time hustlers operating out of their homes after a day's work can be choosier about answering the phone and seeing clients. They already have a salary that pays the rent. As a source of additional income hustling does bring spectacular rewards. This is even true of part-time street hustlers. To the dismay of the regulars, part-timers will take to the street when there is a convention or some such in town. They will do better because they are cleaner, fresher, and more relaxed.

Specialists are hustlers such as bodybuilders or S/M practitioners with great imagination. There are simply not enough of them to go around. Their devoted worshipers will travel thousands of miles to be with them or will fly them cross-country.

SELF-IMAGE ENHANCEMENT

Some hustlers operating out of their homes are remarkably unattractive. How such hustlers develop a steady clientele will be discussed later on. At this point, I want to quote Alex Lim, a short and thin Chinese guy with an underexercised body, a very plain face, bad teeth, and a squeaky voice. He makes up for his physical shortcomings by his friendliness, cooperation, sincere empathy, and, last but not least, very hot, passionate, and, upon request, kinky sex. "Nobody paid attention to me in bars," he told me. "I was never asked to spend the night with anyone. Now that I charge for it, and I charge plenty, the same men are all over me, and there are only so many calls I can handle when I come home from work."

Many street hustlers who appear ugly are often only very scruffy and unkempt. For some clients, this has a charm of its own. But even truly homely hustlers get picked up. This, too, I will discuss later.

An ungainly young man who is lucky enough, on rare occasions, to be chosen by a drunken troll when the bar is about to close needs to work on his self-image. He puts an ad in the paper as a model. A week later, he may be summoned to the elegant home of a client who turns out to be a gorgeous hunk, and who tips him generously at the end of the session. Frogs can turn into princes through the magic of hustling!

SELF-JUSTIFICATION

Many hustlers engage in sex pretending (to themselves) that it is just a job. To legitimize the job, they need to get paid for the sex. The same sexual practices, done recreationally, would make them feel very guilty. Bisexuals make up the largest group of such hustlers.

Donald, a good friend of mine, worships extremely masculine men. He finds his sexual partners among blue-collar workers. He makes contact with them by placing personal ads in straight or semistraight publications. These contacts are people who make good wages and do not really need the extra income Donald provides. However, the money is a handy excuse for engaging in homosexual acts, especially since most of his partners are married men.

Donald enjoys prolonged jack-off sessions. That suits his partners well. They regard these sessions as a throwback to their boyhoods when they jerked off with the other kids. They do not permit any "funny" stuff, such as kissing or going down on each other. Just "boy-to-boy" stuff, while watching heterosexual porno. Nothing queer about that!

After a few encounters, when they feel more comfortable with Donald, some will ask him to buy a dildo and use it on them. (Of course, they cannot keep one at home.) More encounters take place, and then they want to be screwed, penetrated as macho men: no affection, no kissing, or any other romantic nonsense. Donald is not crazy about this development because he really does not want to screw them, but he needs to keep his supermasculine hustlers happy. Then, inevitably, they have a "surprise" for him. Somehow, they contrive to get hold of the cutest drag outfit, and wouldn't he just love to see them put it on? Donald hates it! He is into macho men, not drag queens. But, to keep his blue-collar hustlers interested in the game—they do not really need his money—he permits them to perform their ritual a few times a year.

Or take another illustration. In San Juan, Puerto Rico, many of the hustlers are bisexuals, often married with children. They hang out around gay hotels and make a fair amount of money off the tourists. (Most of it, unfortunately, goes for drugs and booze rather than to feed their children.) In the line of duty, they are very versatile and often extremely passionate. This is OK—they are just doing their job. Done recreationally, for free, it would make them the worst *maricones* on the island.

In the self-justification category, the next group are young guys who need to have sex with older men. To a certain extent, all successful hustlers must be comfortable with older men because the majority of their clients (definitely not all of them) fall into this category. But I single out here young men who have a psychological and physical need to have sex with "mature," or even old, partners.

These young guys who lust after "mature gentlemen"[1] are usually not "public" hustlers. They do not want to be intimate with all sorts of clients but rather with carefully selected older men. The financial arrangement creates the illusion of doing a job, which helps them justify conduct for which they have no explanation, and which is regarded as perverse, at least by the gay community in the United States. (Other societies, e.g., Japanese and Latino, are less uptight about May-December male relationships.)

Interestingly, in this group are many bisexuals with girlfriends their own age. They are completely mystified by their sexual need for older males in addition to their young girlfriends. The money they earn from the geriatric hustling helps them cope with this puzzlement.

One cannot dismiss this behavior, or even a monogamous "sugar daddy" arrangement, simply as an exchange of money for sexual favors. The younger guys must perform sexually: get a hard on, ejaculate, screw, and so on. It is inconceivable that they would be able to fake their own sexual excitement over a period of years!

The last group in the behavior-justification category are hustlers who practice S/M. For two practical reasons, most of them (*not* all) are sadists rather than masochists. First, because the demand is uneven: for every master there seem to be ten slaves. Second, a masochistic hustler puts himself in an extremely vulnerable position.

There are quite a few hustlers who advertise themselves as "masters, spankers, tough punks," etc. Only occasionally does one see ads offering hustler service as a "slave."

Clients are willing to pay for special services (such as being spanked or whipped or pissed on) and hustlers can gain financially by what they enjoy doing in the first place.[2] The masochistic client benefits greatly by establishing the ground rules for the paid scene, rather than taking his chances with an unpaid sadist who may get carried away and inflict serious damage.

Here, too, the vocation enters the picture. Not all hustlers are willing or able to play the role of a sadist. Since S/M is a game, reinvented by the players with each encounter, a reluctant hustler who does not appreciate the complexity of the scene will destroy the illusion by inappropriate behavior.

THE GREAT ADVENTURE

For practical reasons hustlers who advertise their services in newspapers operate their businesses under fictitious names. When they receive phone calls they know immediately whether the calls are personal or business-related. When they run more than one ad, offering different services (e.g., massage and "modeling"), they sometimes use more than one fictitious name.

Even when they are not confronted by such considerations, if, for instance, they are street hustlers, they are likely to operate under a fictitious name. By taking on a name of their choosing and assuming a different identity, they liberate themselves symbolically from the "baggage" that comes with their given name. This is how the adventure starts.

Alfonso, a handsome young Chicano student, would dress sharply when making out calls to the Fairmont and other swank San Francisco hotels. Sometimes, after turning a trick, he would walk boldly into a function room, pretend to be one of the invitees, and treat himself to a free dinner.

I am sure that for Alfonso, AKA Joseph Martinez, the free meal at the Fairmont had great symbolic value. He was born in Salinas, California, into a poor Mexican family, and was unhappy with his Hispanic appearance. Many times in his life he was made to feel very uncomfortable by his brown skin. Once he was even checked out by the Immigration Service, which suspected him of being undocumented. As Joseph Martinez, a sophomore at San Francisco State, he had no business at the Fairmont as guest or invitee. As model Alfonso, he had just finished "conferring" with a Fairmont VIP guest, and his dropping in on another function for a bite to eat raised no eyebrows.

Joseph, qua Joseph, was a nobody to the Fairmont crowd. He had worked at an ice cream parlor before he started his hustling career. At the Fairmont, all he could possibly have been was a busboy. Model Alfonso received (in 1976) $50 plus a generous tip for an hour's work!

Or take another example: Jerry Elgin, a very tall and exceptionally attractive guy, had been a member of the Mensa Society (for people with a high IQ and a large ego) for two years when I met him in 1975. He was a college student and had taken two semesters of French. He planned on visiting France during his summer vacations. Being short on funds, he decided to earn a few francs by hustling in Paris.

Jerry became sexually aroused by just talking about his plan. I said to him once, "Jerry, even if you had $10,000 in your travel fund, you would go through with the hustling plan." He thought for a moment and said, "You're right. It will test my French, that's for damn sure."

He did hustle in France and he was pleased with his Parisian clients, with whom he conversed in French. The few nights he hustled in Paris were the most exciting experiences of his trip.

In what other profession do people work under a code name, and lead a double life? When they are secret agents of some kind. Just as in spy movies, there is sex, adventure, and real danger involved in hustling. For some, this adds to the excitement.

IN-BETWEEN-JOBS HUSTLERS

Almost all full-time street hustlers start hustling as a last-resort or between-jobs measure. For many of them, the last resort becomes a decade-long occupation.

Hustler Andy is a good illustration. He was one of the first hustlers I met in San Francisco. Andy plied his trade from the corner of Market and Mason Streets, which was not as elegant a hustling location as the Geary Street side of the St. Francis Hotel.

Andy, twenty-three-years old at the time, was of Italian descent. He would have been dark and handsome had his nose not been broken and never healed properly. Even with the awkward nose, he was winsome.

He certainly had a vocation for hustling, and was always a good sex partner. As a matter of fact, he *enjoyed* hustling.

I will have more to say about the incongruities and idiosyncrasies of hustlers that make them such interesting characters. Here I'll just mention that Andy would have made Miss Manners proud. He tolerated absolutely no swearing in his presence, not even using the "D" word. He traveled and lived with an allegedly straight pool hustler, whom he supported out of his meager earnings.[3] The pool hustler had a lot of free time on his hands, and spent it reading—what else?—the Bible.

When I first met Andy he told me that he had been looking for a "real" job since arriving in San Francisco a few months earlier, but had not been able to find one. In those days, I still believed that any "honest" job would be preferable to hustling. I tried to help Andy find a job. I spoke to the manager of a car-wash business, who was an acquaintance of a friend of mine, and obtained a note from him that Andy could start working there the following Monday morning at 8 a.m.

Proudly, I told Andy the good news. He looked at me as if I had uttered a string of four-letter words. "I was not born to be a car washer," he told me disdainfully.

I suppressed the logical follow-up question: "Were you born to hustle?" Instead, I asked him, "What job would be acceptable to you?"

"Oh, I don't know. An office job, maybe something in sales . . ."

It took a while before I pieced together the truth. Since graduating from high school in Chicago, Andy had not held any job. He was an itinerant hustler, moving aimlessly from city to city. It was true that jobs in San Francisco were difficult to obtain. But even if jobs had been plentiful, Andy would have been a poor candidate. He had no skills or experience to offer a potential employer. The car-wash job was a good choice for him.

In theory, he could have done better for himself than washing cars. He was always clean and well-groomed, and could easily have started out, for example, as a busboy, working his way up to becoming a waiter. In practice, he would have been fired from any job requiring a good attendance record.

Andy had a lot of trouble keeping his appointments. Bad things always happened to him. At the beginning of one week, he spent twenty-four hours in jail for contributing to the delinquency of a minor girl. (He had been on the premises when his neighbor, at his transient hotel, offered alcohol to a young girl. The charge was dismissed.) In the middle of the week he spent all of his rent money, plus the money he earned for selling his blood,[4] to buy an ornate frame for a painting he had been given by a client. At the end of the same week, he got locked out of his hotel room for not paying the rent, and had no change of clothing.

There is an irony in all of this. Andy was an excellent hustler. Had society left him alone, all he would have needed to worry about would be the same issue that, say, a professional boxer confronts: What will he do with himself once he grows too old for his present profession? (The difference is that boxing is about hurting, whereas hustling is about nurturing!) But, of course, society, including the law, would not leave Andy alone. He had to make, or pretend to make, feeble attempts at finding a regular job. There was no way that he could feel happy just doing what he did best.

The "in between" hustlers take different roads to retire from their hustling careers. The more intelligent ones, or the ones who are not so intelligent but are in charge of their lives, gradually get out of full-time hustling, and, eventually, find a regular job and/or go back to school. I will discuss in the next chapter why getting out of hustling is usually a gradual process.

Some wait until they are forced to retire from hustling due to their age. They end up working in baths, sex clubs, adult book stores, and, in recent years, as caregivers for people with AIDS.

Until the Welfare Reform Act of 1996, one way out was to qualify for Supplemental Security Income (SSI) benefits. These were usually granted for mental problems due to drug-related conditions. How this will play out with the new rules for SSI benefits only time will tell.

While writing this chapter, I have had a paranormal experience of sorts. I have been thinking about a hustler I have not seen for some nine years. I was sure that by now he had died of AIDS, a drug overdose, or another Polk Street mishap. (For instance, during my time in San Francisco, there have been a disproportionate number of gruesome murders in this location.)

I was introduced to Roland through another hustler when he arrived in San Francisco from Seattle, at the age of eighteen. He was a plain-looking Samoan, short, a bit on the chubby side, with a round face full of youthful acne. Roland was a nice guy, but his extreme shyness and his drug habit made him very difficult to converse with. His sexual performance depended on the type and quantity of drugs he had taken earlier in the day. As a result, Roland was an unreliable hustler; a sexual experience with him could turn out to be excellent or very poor. With his drug habit and lack of skills, hustling on the street was the best he could do. For a while, I kept tabs on Roland through the hustler who had introduced me to him, in whose apartment Roland would crash from time to time. Eventually, I lost contact with all street hustlers.

Nine years later, a chubbier, bearded, and bedraggled Roland greeted me with a broad smile, displaying a set of teeth sorely in need of dental care. His acne, like his youth, had disappeared. We had a brief chat. Roland was still hustling, obviously well-nourished and apparently in good health. Maybe it was not an ideal way to live, but, given his limitations, a means to survive! When Roland started hustling, at the age of eighteen, he was, in his own mind, an "in between" hustler. In his case, the "in between" became a permanent occupation.

Chapter 5

Three Kinds of Hustlers

In the beginning there was the street hustler.

Until very recently, both men and women walked the streets if they wanted to sell sex, unless they worked out of a bordello. Some twenty-five years ago the profession was "upgraded." Nowadays, there are three categories of hustlers: the street hustler, the masseur, and the "model" or "escort."

It would be more correct to call street hustlers "public hustlers." These are hustlers who conduct their business where they will be seen by prospective clients. It does not need to be in the street; it can be in a bar or a public building.

In the United States, hustlers usually operate in the streets, such as Polk Street in San Francisco and Santa Monica Boulevard in Hollywood. Guys loitering in these locations will be recognized by prospective clients as hustlers. (Nowadays a homeless person may be mistaken for a hustler.)

In other countries, the street-hustling scene is more subdued. Brazen hustling may be better for business, but I suspect that many hustlers prefer to able to blend into the crowd when it suits them.

When I was last in Barcelona, in 1988, there was a brisk hustling scene in all the gay baths. One could not make any assumptions about who was a hustler. The cutest young guy in the baths turned out to be in the "mili" (doing his national service in the military), and though he hung out with the other hustlers he was not one himself. Hustlers in Barcelona's baths could blend into the general population if needed. For instance, they might run into a friend who did not know about their hustling.

In Manila, a favorite hustling spot is the Harrison Shopping Plaza. The whole plaza is air-conditioned. In torrid Manila, it is a wonderful place to hang out for anyone who wants to escape the heat and do window shopping. A hustler could run into his grand-mother there, without giving away his secret.

In Zurich, hustlers ply their business at the Bahnhof—the central railway station. The Bahnhof is an important commercial center, with many shops and restaurants, as well as a major street-car terminal. It is crowded day and night. It is also a cruising place. Being seen there by friends and relatives would not embarrass a hustler.

Whether the scene is strident or subdued, a hustler working in public is known to his peers, and to the police, if they want to take notice of it. All too often, hustlers fight with each other over terri-tory, drugs, boyfriends, unpaid debts, and so on, or are being harassed by the police. Like female streetwalkers, they also attract a lunatic fringe that is out to inflict physical harm on them.

A lot of bad stuff, with no rhyme or reason, just happens on the street. For instance, I once made a date with Ricky, a hustler whom I had met a few evenings earlier. I was supposed to pick him up at 6 p.m., not far from his street corner. When he did not show up, I parked the car and went cruising on Polk Street. Some ten minutes later I ran into Ricky. "Hey, you stood me up," I said.

"The cops took me to the police station," he said. "Look at my wrists, you can still see the marks of the handcuffs."

"What did you do?"

"Nothing."

"So why did they take you in?"

"Because they are assholes, that's why." He took out a piece of paper. It stated that he had been detained and released with no charges pressed. All in all, he was run in and released in less than an hour.

What was that all about? Periodically, the police come under pressure from merchants to do *something* about hustlers, who block store entrances and are rowdy. In response, the police arrest and charge a number of hustlers, cite others, and harass the rest of them. In the end, it does not change anything. Hustling has been going on in San Francisco since the Gold Rush days and maybe even before that. But the police, like the hustlers and their clients, need to play out their respective roles.

Because life on the street is so unpredictable, street hustlers find it difficult to make any commitments for anything but the immediate present. They may not be able to get any sleep on a particular night and therefore may not show up for a job the next morning; they have difficulties keeping dates made for a specific time on a subsequent day because they may be turning a trick then; they cannot be reached by phone because they do not have one. Many, by no means all, are forever missing their IDs, losing their house keys, and being denied access to their belongings.

If they are full-time hustlers it is next to impossible for them to avoid drugs. Drug deals are made in front of them all the time; clients offer the stuff to them; almost everybody around them is high on something or crashing because something they took is wearing off. And then, of course, there is alcohol.

Yet, more than once, I have heard full-time hustlers describe life on the street as "glamorous." Glamorous? Well, yes, in a strange way. On this very night they might meet a famous actor in Hollywood, an important muck-a-muck in Washington, DC, or a fabulously rich man in New York City. They may be picked up by a gorgeous hunk, have wild sex with lots of cocaine thrown in, or be fussed over and spoiled by a lonely old man who falls in love with them. Such things happen once in a blue moon—but happen they do!

Then there is the freedom of the street. Even though this freedom is mostly illusory, hustlers bask in it. They can sleep until noon, not keep the date they had made the previous day because they already have all the money they need at the moment, and spend their last penny on an expensive trinket they will never use.

There is no neat division between full-time and part-time hustlers.[1] The part-timers are simply hustlers who have a steady source of income not generated by hustling. Many of the part-timers receive (at least prior to the Welfare Reform Act of 1996) welfare assistance, food stamps, or SSI funds. The rest hold some type of a job, and hustle for extra income. Since their exposure to the street is limited, and their living conditions much more stable, they have more control of their lives.

This control is usually related to their relatively stable living conditions. Street hustlers (at least in the United States) tend to move from one slum hotel to the next, renting rooms by the night or the week. (The smarter ones, if they have the money, pay by the month.) To meet the rent deadline (which always seems to be tomorrow at noon!) full-time hustlers must turn tricks *now.* The hustlers' tension, when trying to clinch the sale in order to pay the rent, spooks some clients. The part-time hustlers, with a secure living place, have an easier time of it.

For many other reasons, part-time hustlers tend do better on the street than the full timers. They are cleaner, more relaxed, and they are in a position to make and keep future appointments with their clients. Eventually, with enough regulars, they do not need to spend much time on the street. The greatest achievement of street hustlers is to become part-time hustlers.

Without permanent living quarters, full-time hustlers are without a phone and a mailing address. This makes it all but impossible for them to find a job even if they want to do so. If they somehow manage to find one, they have tremendous difficulties in coordinating their erratic hustling hours with their job schedule.

I have known a lot of hustlers who received some sort of welfare. The "elite" manage to receive SSI, almost always for being mentally ill. Their mental condition is usually not reflected in their sexual performance. The following anecdote is a good illustration.

I met Peter when he was twenty-eight years old. He was an ethnic mixture of Native American, Filipino, and African, and was very handsome. Unfortunately, he had a sweet tooth, and was on his way to becoming seriously chubby. I liked him for his cheerful disposition and for his lustful, yet gentle and caring, sexuality. He reminded me of the hippies of yore, always speaking of love and peace, and using expressions like "groovy." Though he was a street hustler, sometimes even homeless, he was quite good about keeping appointments. I knew he did a lot of drugs but that was usual for a guy in his circumstances.

One day he called me from the psychiatric ward of San Francisco General. He begged me to visit him there. As soon as I was let through the security door, Peter grabbed me and, kissing me passionately, waltzed me into a private visiting cubicle. I was somewhat embarrassed by the spectacle we made, but, after all, it was a mental ward where patients were expected to behave strangely. In a psychiatric ward, being kissed by Peter was not the worst thing that could have happened to me. Later, I found out from the nurse that I was his only visitor. Apparently, he tried to show the other patients that he, too, had friends.

He had been committed for observation. A few days earlier, under the influence of drugs, he had disturbed the peace by yelling at passers-by, including a police sergeant. He was released after a few days. During our next sex session he was even more passionate than before. Maybe this was his way of repaying me for my visit.

A month later, he wound up at the hospital once again. This time, as a condition for not pressing charges or committing him, he had to agree to live in a halfway house for nine months. I would pick him up there between his three mandatory daily meetings. "What happens at these meetings?" I asked.

"We talk about not using."

"Not using what?"

He was surprised by my lack of worldliness. "Drugs, Joseph!"

"What else do you talk about?"

"What else is there to talk about?"

"The future. Didn't you tell me once that you had never held a job? What happens once you are out on your own?"

"Well, all they talk about is not using, even if you feel like using."

"Don't they try to teach you a skill you can use after the program is over?"

"No, Joseph! We just talk about not using. How we have low self-esteem because we use. How we screw up our lives because we use."

I felt that Peter was somewhat exasperated with my questions about the future.

For a while, Peter was on antipsychotic medication. As a side effect, he was unable to climax. This depressed him, though it did not affect his horniness. When he was with me, he appeared completely sane.

But now that he had fallen into the hands of the psychiatric profession, he spun the web that would allow him to trap the biggest catch of all: SSI benefits for the rest of his life! He accomplished his goal in just six months. From then on, his living and medical expenses would be covered by the state, and his hustling money would go for drugs. He deserted the halfway house and moved to

San Diego. I lost touch with him. Mostly likely, he is still collecting his benefits, hustling, and using drugs.

What many street hustlers sorely lack are skills that would help them find regular jobs. Merely teaching them how "not to use" leaves them no choice but to go back to the one skill they do have. Once they go back to hustling they will "use," because that is the way things are on the street. The drug-related SSI just assures them of a small pension for the rest of their lives.

Two observations based solely on my own experiences: First, there is absolutely no connection between a hustler's diagnosed mental condition and his sexual performance and, indeed, his ability to conduct his sex business. Second, the crazier the hustler, the less likely he is to collect benefits. My only explanation for this phenomenon is that social workers prefer working with pleasant clients, and leave the really crazy ones to fend for themselves.

* * *

I know quite a bit about the massage business from both the client's and the masseur's point of view. Once, for a period of some six months, I had a housemate who made his living as a masseur. He was from Mexico, and, in the beginning, hardly spoke any English. I was often called in to interpret during phone negotiations. After giving a massage, he would share his experiences with me. But before discussing masseurs, let me start with a brief historical overview.

When I was a student in New York City, in the 1950s, I was friends with a young woman who studied Swedish massage. I remember that she had to know a lot of anatomy, and that she apprenticed in a hospital. When she graduated, she ran an ad in the yellow pages, advertising her services as a Swedish masseuse. All of the callers were men, and most of them wanted some sort of sex. The one or two clients she did see, harassed her. After a few months she changed her telephone number and gave up her business.

I write this because I believe that masseuses and, later, masseurs, were the "pioneers" of today's sex workers who operate out of their homes. I am sure that Swedish massage, per se, had no connection with the sex trade. It was the advertised phone numbers of masseuses operating from their homes, and the almost nude massage that eroticized the profession. The Swedish masseuses did not become prostitutes. Rather, prostitutes became masseuses.

Swedish massage is somewhat austere and dour. It is meant to be therapeutic, not touchy-feely. In the 1960s, the Human Potential Movement introduced other types of massage. The most famous style, Esalen massage, was born at Big Sur (a few hours' drive south of San Francisco). These types of massage, while not sexual, were supposed to be sensual. The emphasis was on intimacy between the massage giver and the recipient, rather than on therapy. The massage was intended to make recipients feel good instead of only improving their health.

Massage schools were established to teach practitioners the new massage styles. Though these various styles were not meant to be sexual in nature, the very strict protocol of Swedish massage—always covering and *ignoring* the genital area—was dispensed with.

These new massage techniques coincided with gay publications that featured descriptive advertisements for various services. Out of this union was born the "massage" section in the classified ads. Following are three illustrations that tell the story.

1. This is a massage ad only, it does not matter how attractive I am. It does not matter how hung you are.[2]

2. EROTIC 24 HOURS
   CMT Massage[3]

3. X-Defined, X-Lean, X-Safe
   FULL RELEASE
   Pro-frontal massage by nude stallion boy
   Smooth, young, dark-haired, bubble-butt, hung
   $50+ outcalls/hotels[4]

Masseur number 1 is a marvelous example of the frustrations a "legitimate" massage practitioner has to endure. All he wants to do is to make his living giving massages. (We know that he is a licensed masseur because he advertises in a classified section titled *Licensed Massages.*) However, his clients insist that he perform more than a massage. In his short ad he describes two of his clients' sales pitches for more than just a massage: (a) You are such a good-looking guy. What a shame to waste it on just massaging me; (b) I am so well-hung, baby, that you *want* to do more than just give me a dumb massage. This masseur is so obsessed with not wanting to perform sexual "enhancements" that, in the process, he forgets to tell what sort of a massage he does offer.

I have no quarrel with masseur number 1. Every practitioner is entitled to give the massage he wants. Unfortunately for him, he will be penalized by his clients for his choice. Nonsexual masseurs, regardless of the quality of their massage, make a lot less than the ones who, such as masseur number 2, give an erotic massage.

What is an "erotic massage?" Well, it is synonymous with a "release massage" or a "full-body massage." In plain English, sometime during the massage, the masseur jerks the client off, or massages him while the client masturbates on his own.

For whatever it is worth, here is my take on all of this: Were it not for religious squeamishness—equating ejaculation with sin—*all* masseurs would "release" their clients if the latter wanted it. Massage is supposed to be a *relaxing* experience and many men feel more relaxed after ejaculating. *Personally,* I do not see the difference between massaging toes and fingers and handling a penis.

From his ad one understands tacitly that masseur number 2 is willing to bring the client to a climax. What else he is willing to do is discretionary. The ad is confusing, but it is meant to be so. Masseur number 2 deliberately straddles the line between a massage professional and a sex worker. His clients deliberately straddle the line between remunerating a legitimate professional, and paying for sex. Paradoxically, all of this works to the disadvantage of genuine masseurs. They are paid less than hustlers while working much harder physically. This paradox leads us to the third ad.

Masseur number 3 is willing to give an erotic massage to those who are satisfied with just that (he uses both "release" and "frontal" to make sure that even the dullest reader would get his drift) but, if a client wants more, number 3 has it all: defined, lean, handsome, and hung! Of course, the clients need to understand that the fees are $50 and up depending on the extras thrown in by the masseur. With his "bubble butt" who knows where all of this will end!

It is worth noting that masseur number 3 also claims to be a "pro." Massage, unlike hustling, is not so much a vocation as a skill that can be learned. In the best of all possible worlds, the client will get a handsome, young, hung, *well-trained* masseur. But we do not live in a perfect world. It is rare that the cute and sexy masseur knows a lot about the massage part of his craft. I have been massaged by very cute masseurs whose massage was either like an S/M encounter somewhat beyond my limits, or an annoying tickling session administered by clumsy fingers.

Sexual massages are all too often frustrating to both the masseur and the client. A trained masseur strains himself less physically than an amateur, because he has studied techniques to conserve his energy. But as soon as he has gone through the training, which is long and expensive, the masseur feels (or is brainwashed) that, as a professional, he need not provide sexual services . . . at least, not beyond "release." The untrained masseur, who is physically exhausted after two or three clients, wants to get it over with as fast as possible by making the client climax without much massaging. For this, he is willing to take some shortcuts.

Because of the ambiguity of the massage business the ground rules need to be established before the session. Otherwise, the client is likely to get less (sometimes more!) than he expects. I will discuss later, in *precise* detail, how to negotiate, on the phone, with a prospective masseur.

Very good masseurs with sex appeal, who are willing to stretch the massage envelope a bit (e.g., allow clients to blow them a little just before coming) can make a reasonable living. They tend to have repeat business, and educate their clients to make appointments in advance and at reasonable hours. Masseurs can, and do, engage in their profession much longer than hustlers.

* * *

Operating a hustling business out of one's home is a relatively new phenomenon that started in the 1970s. It has been made possible by publications that are willing to accept descriptive ads about the services provided by hustlers. Answering machines and, later, pagers and cellular telephones, have made it possible for hustlers to run their businesses out of their homes in an *efficient* manner. The new venue also raised the acceptable age for hustlers. Guys in their forties advertise on a regular basis as "models," though one rarely sees them hustling on the street.

I consider myself very lucky to have witnessed the upgrading of the hustling profession—from street hustlers to models working out of their homes. Other professionals change their title when they upgrade their services. For instance, the lowly chiropodists who used to cut toenails and remove corns and calluses upgraded themselves to podiatrists—foot doctors—within my lifetime. Hustlers becoming models is fine with me.

Following are two illustrations demonstrating why I consider this upgrading such a boon to the gay community.

Within the last two years I traveled to London and to Honolulu. Both times I was with friends. For a number of reasons, cruising was not on our agenda, although sexual encounters were very much on my individual agenda. What I wanted was to make an in call, that is, visit the hustler at his residence.

In Honolulu, a limited number of models were listed in the local gay publication. The first guy I spoke to appeared to be a good match. For a daytime in call he charged $80. He lived in Waikiki, one block away from the beach, in a high-security building. The only way I was going to get into the building was for him to admit me personally, after I signed in with the security guard! He lived in a spacious one-bedroom apartment, very tastefully decorated.

His elegant accommodations really surprised me. I had been in Honolulu many times. In the 1960s and 1970s I ran around with quite a few *kama'aima* (locals). For mysterious reasons, I was very popular with them and had no need to resort to hustlers. They were all guys who worked in the tourist industry. I was in many of their homes. Rents were very high, and they had to share their austere accommodations with roommates. And now here is a model operating out of such elegant quarters.

The model, Glenn, was a tall guy, originally from mainland China, in his late twenties. He was not exactly my type. I looked around the living room and saw a large computer, a laptop, and computer floppies strewn all over the desk. In addition to being a model, Glenn was an independent computer consultant. He found out that I had been a hypnotherapist until a few years earlier. The result was an animated conversation. I asked him about computers, and he wanted to know more about hypnosis. We talked for at least half an hour before entering his bedroom.

It mattered little that he was not exactly my type. From our phone conversation he knew what I wanted, and he performed his part competently and in a caring way. Before I left he gave me a card with his phone and fax numbers, as well as his e-mail address.

In London, where there were lots of model listings in the gay paper, it took some ten phone calls before I found someone with whom I thought I would be compatible, and whose fees I could afford. Arthur, originally from Barbados, was a dancer by profession. We agreed on a fee that converted into U.S. $83. He was willing to give me a discount because the taxi ride to his place was an expensive proposition.

Arthur lived in a small flat, in a somewhat shabby house. Soon enough I forgot all about Arthur's living circumstances and concentrated on him. He was a strikingly handsome black man in his early thirties, and had one the most beautiful bodies I had ever been intimate with! He had a perfect dancer's build: strong and lean, with supple, rather than bulging, muscles. Unlike his Hawaiian colleague, he was not a great conversationalist. He undressed me immediately, and, by way of starting the session, gave me a back rub. Then we really had a wild session.

It came as no surprise to me that both models were excellent sexual partners who had a vocation for their profession. This is true of most models. Street hustlers can be selective of their clients, just as much as the clients can pick and choose their hustlers. A street hustler can walk away from a client he does not like. The model is stuck with whomever he made the appointment, including clients who are drunk or on drugs or just obnoxious. Models are psychologically better prepared to satisfy their clients. As a rule, when a model both knows in advance what the client's needs are, and agrees to satisfy them, he will do a good job. In my experience, it is rare that a model will turn out to be a sexual dud.

In both Honolulu and London I could have found a street hustler. It would have taken much longer, and then the sex might have been inadequate. (But a hand-picked hustler, unlike a model, would be *certain* to be my physical type!) Also, picking up a street hustler always entails a certain amount of danger. By making an in call to the model's home this danger is all but eliminated.

With all the advantages that models offer, how is it that street hustlers are still in demand, even in large metropolitan areas where there are many sex ads?

Why one person is sexually attracted to another is a matter of sexual chemistry. (Not a scientific term, but we all know how it works.) Sometimes, the chemistry is not there even though, in theory, it ought to be. For instance, an ad reading:

> Tall, slim, muscular, well-hung blond, blue eyes,
> 30 y/o, versatile, aims to please, in/out calls.

may turn you on. You talk to the guy on the phone, everything clicks into place, and you make a date for an out call. Then, when he arrives at your home, you just do not feel any chemistry. By then it is difficult to back out. This lack of instant chemistry simply could not happen with a street hustler whom you see and talk to in person.

The client's disappointment upon visual inspection is frequently created by the model's statements over the telephone. Sometimes there is an honest difference of perception. What one person describes as an "athletic body" may seem thin and underexercised to another. But very often hustlers' statements are outright lies to clinch a sale. (Counterproductively, some clients lie to their prospective hustlers, a subject I will take up later.)

In my experience the lies are mostly age-related. The reason is that age is in the eye of the beholder, whereas height, weight, skin color, length of penis, etc., are factual observations. Street hustlers lie when they are underage.[5] Models almost always shave a few years off. Sometimes they pretend to be even younger than they are. A twenty-two-year-old might claim to be twenty. It does get serious when models understate their age by fifteen years!

Summing it all up, models have expanded the hustling universe. They have added tremendous variety, accessibility, and professionalism. However, the beeper and voice mail, unlike the answering machine, have made model in calls somewhat *less* safe than they used to be. This subject will be discussed in Chapter 12.

Chapter 6

How Hustlers Price Their Services

To know how to work out a mutually beneficial deal with a hustler, you need to understand the finances involved in the hustling trade. Most full-time street hustlers, and quite a few models, do not have the faintest idea of how much they earn per year, or even per month.

When reporters interview hustlers, the latter are likely to state that they make $400 a day, or some such. Working five days a week, and taking two weeks off for a well-deserved vacation, will give these hustlers a cool annual income of $100,000. So how come they have no money to pay for a hotel room for the night?

There are, indeed, days when hustlers make $400, and even more. But there are also days on end when they earn very little, or nothing at all. Full-time hustlers are loathe to admit that they barely eke out a living because, inevitably, they will be asked, "So why do you hustle?"

Not only do they not keep books, but whatever money they make seems to evaporate. The Costa Rican transvestite hustler I mentioned in Chapter 3 explained this by saying, *"Dinero malo sale rapido"* (bad money is swiftly spent). In her case, just her drag outfits and makeup consumed most of her earnings. The rest probably went for drugs.

In addition to drugs, alcohol, expensive hotel rooms (rented on a daily basis at a premium), and constant eating out, many hustlers get rid of their earnings by acquiring a lot of stuff they definitely do not need. The more impractical the item, the more likely it is to be bought by a hustler.

I know one hustler who bought a very elegant and expensive three-piece suit for himself. He never used it, because it would have been completely inappropriate attire for hustling. Since he moved from one hotel to another, he had to store the suit at a friend's home. Finally, many months after having bought the suit, the day arrived when he could wear it—unfortunately, to a funeral. That was the day after he had had a fight with his friend, who would not let him come by to pick up the suit.

With a lot of money on their hands, experienced hustlers will pay rent in advance. But they usually do not have a place to park the rest of the cash. Most of them do not have bank accounts, and they are afraid to carry a lot of money or to have friends keep it for them. The impractical things they purchase can be stored at friends' homes, with some assurance that the things will be returned to them.

Hustlers deal with unreal money. One moment they are hungry, homeless, and broke. Two hours later, they have $150 to burn! The next day they will be on the same corner—hungry, homeless, and broke—easy come, easy go. It does not really matter how much these hustlers earn per month or per annum, because, in the end, they have little to show.

All of this is different for part-time street hustlers and models. By just having places to live, and not hanging out in the street at all hours, they have more control over their finances. With them, money really adds up. A number of them even manage to put themselves through college.

Frustratingly for all hustlers and models, in the beginning they almost always do better than later on in their careers. A new face on the street or a different ad in the paper attracts attention. This beginners' luck evaporates after a while. Unfortunately, hustlers and models tend to remember the olden days that may never be repeated.

* * *

Of the three kinds of hustlers, only the compensation of masseurs has a logical, economic basis. Disappointingly for them, they are paid less per session than hustlers. It is disappointing because, in addition to working very hard, they have a substantial overhead. For in calls they need to maintain a decent space. (Models can and do get away with shabbier accommodations!) They have to provide sheets, towels, and oil. Professional masseurs, and those who want to have less hanky-panky with clients, require a massage table. Their constant overhead is the weekly ads they must place in the gay press.

In San Francisco an hour's worth of a nonsexual massage by a CMT (Certified Massage Therapist) costs around $35, as of this writing. A full-body "release" massage runs around $50. Very cute masseurs go as high as $60; older practitioners charge around $40. Sexual "enhancements" by the masseur will be reflected in the tip.

Such an orderly market is of great advantage to clients. Within a narrow band, they can choose between similar providers.

* * *

No such orderly and efficient market exists in the street. Understanding how street hustlers price their services is not easy. It is equally difficult to make sense of the remuneration their clients are willing to offer. A lot of noneconomic issues come into the equation. Guilt (as in "the wages of sin"), low or inflated self-esteem of hustlers and clients, justified worries and neurotic paranoia, and other confusing factors, all play a role in which hustler is chosen and how much he is paid. Two hypothetical illustrations follow:

A street hustler, I'll call him Jerry, starts his shift on a Saturday evening, at 9 p.m. He just spent his last dollar on dinner. He is determined to make, at the *very* least, $75 that night. When he is done, he can rent a cheap hotel room for $35 and finally get a good night's sleep. He owes $25 to another hustler who is going to kick ass if he does not pay him back by tomorrow. With the remaining $15 dollars he can eat the next day.

Jerry showered, shaved, and put on decent clothes at a friend's apartment. His asking price is $90. This is slightly higher than the asking price on the street. But on this particular evening Jerry feels good about himself. He knows that he is an attractive guy, and expects the client to pay top dollar for the privilege of having sex with him.

It turns out to be one of *those* nights. The few assholes who talk to him insult him by offering him only $50. Not a single serious client deigns even to look at him. A regular client who usually picks him up, or at least greets him, ignores him completely. He is interested in a new hustler.

By 2:30 a.m. Jerry is demoralized. The bars have closed and the good potential clients have already picked their choices for the evening, or gone home by themselves. Now Jerry is willing to come down from $90 to $50 because, it stands to reason, the client will ask him to stay the night. He'll save $35 on the hotel room and will be OK financially. By 3:30 a.m., Jerry is desperate. Now he will go with the client for $40, and at 4:00 a.m. for $25.

At 2:05 a.m., a part-time hustler, I'll call him Jim, leaves the bar across the street from where Jerry stands. He did not hook up with anyone at the bar, and is willing to spend a little time trying his luck at picking up a paying gentleman.

Jim has a decent job that pays the bills, but this month he needs extra cash. His asking price is $80, and he has decided that he will not go down in price. He does not want to stay the night with a client (if he has to, he wants to be paid $125), and he is certain that the client will give him cab fare if he does not want to drive him home.

Now, at 2:30 a.m., Jerry at $50 is a much better deal for a potential client. He is much cuter than Jim, and his asking price is $30 less. But Jerry is jinxed on this particular night. He is too anxious to close the deal and get off his feet. When a potential client stops to speak to him, he becomes anxious and sends out tense vibes, which the client interprets as a danger signal. In addition, Jerry insists that the client put him up for the night. For $50, this seems to be too good a deal and raises suspicions.

Up the street, Jim, with four beers under his belt, stands relaxed and confident. It would be nice if he could make some extra money tonight. But he is getting sleepy and he can always try his luck on the street Sunday afternoon. When potential clients talk to him, he is inflexible about his fee and is reluctant to stay the night with them. From Jim, clients get cocky but safe vibes. He may not be as cute as the guy down the street, but better safe than sorry. The client who eventually picks up Jim had spoken briefly to Jerry. He is willing to pay $30 more for a hustler who is not very attractive, and who won't stay the night with him, because he has a funny feeling about Jerry.

At 4:30 Jerry finally gets picked up. His date is a man who lives in a welfare hotel, that is, General Assistance pays his rent. All he can do for Jerry is to put him up for the night and let him sleep late. He has no cash at all to give Jerry, but he'll share his drugs with him.

In such a nonstandardized market, the client can do the same: decide how much he would be willing to pay for a hustler on a particular evening, and stick to his guns. With perseverance, he will find what he is looking for.

* * *

In theory, the models' market should be very orderly and efficient. Clients have access to the fees of all models. If the fee is not printed in the ad, a phone call will make this information available. In practice, the models' market is even more nonstandardized than that of street hustlers.

Unlike hustlers, models have a constant overhead: the ads they insert whenever they have the money for it. Large ads and photographs make ads more expensive.[1] A model's overhead will always be reflected in the fees he charges. However, *there is no relationship between the size of the ad and the sexual competency of the model.*

In the street, hustlers offer more or less similar services. In the ads, models offer a tremendous variety of services. In the street, there are ten or twenty hustlers at a given time. In gay publications of metropolitan areas, there may be hundreds of ads to choose from.

Do you remember the Nasty Pisser (advertiser number 4) in Chapter 2? How did he arrive at $125 for an act many hustlers would offer as a complimentary service? Well, there is no "Pissers of America Guild" with whom he could have consulted before setting his fees, and there is no licensing board for his profession to certify his pissing competency. A basic economics course will teach you that the marketplace will force him to come up with a competitive price, if he wants to be successful in his business. But, if he has a job, he may not care how well his business is doing. If he sees only two clients a month he has already covered the expense of his ads and has made close to $200 in profit. He will not go below the $125 and, as far as he is concerned, the competition be damned. Other models are willing to do a lot more and charge a lot less, because they have to make enough money to cover their rent. In the same market, then, there may be two tiers of models' fees for similar services.

A good question to ask here is why any client would pay the Pisser $125. There are two reasons for it.

First, a lot of clients would be embarrassed to ask an ordinary model to piss on them. They are afraid that they will be rejected out of hand or, worse, be ridiculed by him. Second, clients hope that the Pisser will have an appropriate shtick to go with the pissing act. That would make the experience more . . . meaningful.

In such a market, the client can predetermine what he is willing to pay a model. (Due to the models' fixed overhead, it needs to be higher than the fee for a street hustler.) How to go through ads with this approach will be discussed in a later chapter.

I respect models and have done extremely well for myself using their services. However, I have always felt that their financial expectations (with the notable exception of masseurs) are completely off the wall. *In this, they are aided and abetted by their clients' low self-esteem.*

As I have already written, I shared my home for a while with a Mexican masseur named Jacinto. Jacinto charged $50 for an hour's worth of massage, including the "release" procedure. Jacinto was very cute but mostly mute. At the beginning, he spoke hardly any English. He was twenty-six at the time, though he looked considerably younger. In his entire life, he had been given one hour's instruction in massage techniques.

Before the "grand opening" of his new business he held a dress rehearsal. I was his guinea pig. When he was done, I evaluated the massage. I pointed out that his touch had not been firm enough, and that he had faltered at the critical R minus 10 seconds. Without my own hand's intervention, a release-failure nonevent would have occurred. Jacinto never really got the hang of it, and his clients always had to help him along.

Jacinto's second client was a middle-aged man named Leo. He was a very pleasant, relatively good-looking guy, who could have benefited from joining a gym to lose some weight and tone his flabby muscles.

After Leo left, Jacinto showed me a crisp $100 bill. "Look, he gave me a $50 tip," he said excitedly.

"Did you go *beyond* the release?"

"Joseph, I swear, he got the same massage I gave you the day before yesterday. He had to help me when it came to the climaxing."

"Will he see you again?"

"He already made a date for next week."

"Then we should refer to him as Don Leo." *Don* is a Spanish honorific for very important or distinguished persons. The new appellation stuck.

Don Leo became Jacinto's regular, and even I got to know him pretty well. He saw Jacinto at least once a week and always gave him $100. Jacinto found out later that he saw other masseurs and models as well, and paid the masseurs the same $100. What he gave "models" Jacinto never found out. I suspect it was close to $200.

Don Leo was not a rich person. He could afford to be so generous because he held two full-time supervisory jobs at brokerage houses. One of them probably paid for his massage expenses. I have often tried to figure out what went on in Don Leo's mind. Did he think he was fat and ugly and try to make up for it by doubling the masseurs' fees? Did he feel sorry for the younger masseurs who had to knead his flabby flesh? Did he feel inadequate because he needed to pay for being jerked off? Did he want the masseurs to like him more than their other clients? Did he want to dazzle masseurs with his nonexistent wealth? Finally, did he want to impress the masseurs with his generosity so they would become his lovers?

Since I never discussed these issues with Don Leo—I was not going to ruin things for Jacinto—I do not know the answers. I suspect that all of the above speculations played some role. In the end, Don Leo got the same massage that all other clients received. Once, by way of thanking Don Leo for the outrageously expensive Christmas gifts (plural) that he had given Jacinto, they changed roles. Leo gave Jacinto a massage, and, on that occasion, blew him for a few minutes.

Most, though not all, other clients gave Jacinto tips. Usually, the tips far exceeded the customary 15 percent. In spite of all the generous tips, Jacinto did not make a lot of money from his massage business. Typically, very busy weeks were followed by dry spells. On top of it, Jacinto was unwilling to sit by the phone and wait for clients to call him at odd hours. But when he did make money it was, at times, impressive. One Saturday night he made $325 in four hours. Pretty soon he thought that "releasing" a client, even if performed somewhat ineptly, *ought* to command a large monetary reward.

Had I been able to speak frankly to Don Leo, I would have told him, "Don Leo, don't feel sorry for Jacinto. When he gives you a massage he always listens to tapes of his favorite music. You are kind to him, and there are no supervisors to push him around. Had he worked as an orderly in a hospital, one of the few types of menial jobs he may have been able to secure, he would also have very close physical contact with men—most of them very sick. He would work without the music, the kindness, and the $100 bills. He would be harassed by all kinds of supervisors and argue with co-workers. It would take him two eight-hour shifts to make what you give him for an hour's worth of work!

"Also, Don Leo, you are not the only gay person without a lover. Other gay men go to public restrooms to get the same sex you obtain from Jacinto. Your way is safer, more personal, sanitary, and elegant. But, you say, "I have to pay for it; they get it for free!' Yes, that is true. But consider the fact that the person bringing you to a climax is personable, cheerful, and cute. You got to choose him! In the restroom the guy who jerks you off may well be dirty and ugly. So forget the money and count your blessings!

"Now, then, Don Leo. If you insist on tipping Jacinto and other masseurs, add another $10. This represents a generous 20 percent tip. Get a life, Don Leo. You don't need to work two jobs so that you can overwhelm masseurs and models with your generosity. And, Don Leo, if you want to find a lover, advertise in the personals of a gay publication. Sex workers are professionals. They are not supposed to become lovers!"

With no disrespect whatsoever, I compare the hiring of a hustler or model to the buying of a used car. In the used car business, each deal is unique. You can get a good deal to suit your budget, but you need to look hard for it!

* * *

Before I close this chapter, I would like to discuss how hustlers and models are chosen by their clients.

Anywhere in the world, if you go to places where street hustlers congregate, you will see very few good-looking guys, a lot of ordinary-looking hustlers, and quite a number of homely dudes, sometimes including "physically challenged" ones. Mind you, I am not speaking about hustlers who look like punks or plain bad-ass guys. This image is deliberately cultivated by some hustlers because it is prized by their clients.

At any given time, only a limited number of hustlers are in the street or the bar. Out of that limited number, only three may interest a client. One may be disqualified because he is not sexually compatible, and the other because he charges too much. This leaves only one candidate. He has a few attractive features, appears to be a friendly guy, the price is right, and there definitely is sexual compatibility. But, unfortunately, he is far from handsome.

The client has three choices: pick him up, hang out for another hour and wait for more options, or call it quits for the evening. More often than not, the far-from-handsome guy will be picked up by the client.

My experience, which I am sure is shared by many other clients, has been that I do better with hustlers who are not Adonises. For one, perfect hunks and beautiful queens are sometimes conceited and difficult. For another, we tend to overlook the bad qualities and make excuses for the shortcomings of partners who are exactly our type. *There is absolutely no relationship between good looks and sexual performance.* Most clients find this out sooner or later and go with what is available in the street, even if the packaging is less than perfect.

The model scene presents a set of different problems. Almost always, clients are happily or unhappily surprised by the real models compared to the way they imagined them during the phone interview.

What usually happens when a client is not particularly impressed with the model (but also not entirely disappointed) is that he goes with the flow. The model is already at the client's home, or the latter has already spent time driving and parking on an in call. The client might as well go on with it! Again, given a chance, the frog may turn out to be a prince of a model. Only rarely do models abort the mission. They do not want to lose their time investment. Street hustlers get rid of clients they do not like much more often—provided, of course, that they are not desperate.

It is ironic that hustlers and models who would be ignored in bars and shunned in sex clubs can charge for what they cannot give away for free!

Chapter 7

Taking Control of Your Sex Life

Attempting to control hustlers or models is as practical as trying to use mercury for sculpting. Hustlers and models are all about *not* being controlled by anyone—all too often, not even by themselves. If you must control another person, a lover is a much better prospect. When you hire hustlers, you pay for their services, not for running their lives. Their services will help you control your *own* sexual life!

Hiring hustlers has never been considered an acceptable alternative to endless and frequently futile cruising. I think there are two reasons for this. First, to our great detriment, we gays draw comparisons between our sexual relationships and those of heterosexuals. We compare hustlers to female prostitutes. I have already written enough about this subject. Second, hiring hustlers destroys the romantic illusion we indulge in when cruising.

I have gone to gay bathhouses a thousand times or more. Half my experiences there were dismal. Either I did not score at all, or got it on with men I did not care for (who did not care for me either) just so I could finally escape from the baths and get on with my real life. Some forty-five percent of my baths forays have ranged from mediocre to somewhat adequate. The remaining five percent have been incredibly fulfilling experiences on many levels!

Examples of the five percent: I met my first lover at the baths. Some thirty years ago, at a San Francisco bathhouse, I got it on with a guy from Mexico City, and we are still close friends. The most lucrative summer job I have ever held I obtained through a man I met at the baths. The best sex I have ever had in my entire life was at a gay bathhouse in Vancouver, British Columbia, with a visitor from Seattle. It is, of course, for these five percent that I went (still go, sometimes) to the baths.

I gave all of these examples, because even though I think that bathhouses are hostile cruising grounds, and that they drain time, energy, and money, it *is* possible to have romantic and social encounters there. The same generalizations hold true for bars. In contrast, using the services of hustlers, by definition, negates a romantic relationship. Every time we go cruising most of us hope and pray that we would find more than casual sex—even though we know that this is unlikely. Every time we make a date with a hustler we affirm to ourselves our lustfulness. We know, beforehand, that he would not become a boyfriend or a lover.

But will the hustler just assuage our desire for raw sex or also our yearning for affection? Already in 1976, C.A. Tripp, in his pioneering work, *The Homosexual Matrix*, observed that promiscuity—as in cruising—and affection can and do go hand in hand, at least for a large group of cruisers.[1] If you seek affection from your sex partner (not everybody does) a good hustler will do as well, or even better, than a casual pickup. Even more important, the hustler option will be more efficient than the casual pickup. Only the romantic illusion won't be there.

If we start out with the premise (which we have inherited from heterosexuals) that in order to be a fulfilled gay human being one must have a committed sexual relationship with only one other gay man, then, of course, consorting with hustlers is a problem, not a solution. If, on the other hand, we honor our lustfulness (which exists regardless of whether we honor or dishonor it), then hustlers are a viable solution for *some* gay men.

* * *

I ought to write a bit more about lust and affection, because the whole point of this book is that good hustlers can provide affection to clients who want it. First, we need to be honest with ourselves. Much gay sex takes place *by choice* to satisfy raw lust. A recent issue of the *San Francisco Frontiers News Magazine* features some 400 personal ads. These ads come under three headings: *Relationships, Cruising,* and *Raunch*. Only one-quarter of the ads are listed under *Relationships*. The rest of the advertisers chose to place their ads under *Cruising* and *Raunch*.[2] These advertisers must know from experience that casual sex—as opposed to dating, going steady, and culminating with tying the knot—can be a very satisfying experience.

Were I a poet, I would compose an "Ode to Lust." Lacking the skill, I will recount a personal anecdote.

LUST CONQUERS ALL

My first trip to Japan took place in the summer of 1967. I had read a lot about the country but had not yet studied Japanese. I relied on the (very erroneous) information that everybody in Japan spoke some English.

I arrived in Tokyo early in the morning local time. By dinner time I was tired and irritable due to jet lag. At 9 p.m., I took a taxi to a gay bar. Before entering, I stood outside to clear my head for a while. The cutest Japanese guy, apparently also on his way to the bar, stopped right in front of me. He did not display a broad, friendly smile, which would have run counter to Japanese etiquette. But I interpreted his stare as a "can we get it on" look, and I, not bound by strict etiquette, grinned broadly.

"My name is Joseph," I said, bowing more or less properly.

He replied, "My name is Watanabe," and bowed at the proper angle.

I extended my right hand and said profoundly: "Watanabe *san!*"

He extended his hand. As we shook hands he tried, unsuccessfully, to repeat my name, adding *san* to it.

We stood there for a while shaking each other's hands. When we finally disengaged our hands, I came up with something even more profound to say. "My first day in Japan."

"I . . . no English speak," said Watanabe *san*, pointing at his nose. (This is the emphatic form in Japanese for "I.")

"I do not speak Japanese," said I.

From there on, the quality of our conversation deteriorated. I grew panicky. I was afraid that he would tire of me and disappear into the bar. I was really too tired to follow him and try to cruise him there. I needed to say something that would be understood readily, and convey my intention. I stayed at the Dai Ichi Hotel. I remembered that the Japanese word for hotel was hoteru. I looked straight into his soulful eyes and said, "Dai Ichi Hoteru. We go!"

Right on cue, a taxi drove by. I hailed it, and holding onto Watanabe's elbow guided him into it. During the long, silent ride, I kept worrying about the prominent sign at the Dai Ichi's lobby, right by the elevators, in English and Japanese: "No visitors past this point." I was willing to ignore it; but would Watanabe *san?*

We stepped boldly into the elevator. I do not know whether Watanabe *san* had seen the sign, and, like me, chose to ignore it.

My hotel room was tiny, with only one spartan chair. Without talking, we took off our clothes and hopped into bed.

I had read a lot about how different the Japanese way of thinking was from the Western world's; how difficult it was to communicate with them; how complex their customs were. Watanabe and I spoke eloquently and lovingly, using body language, and we intuited each other's desires. Our agenda was to pleasure ourselves by pleasing each other.

Somehow, he managed to communicate to me that he was a visitor in Tokyo from Nagoya. During our long and very passionate sex session, I did not entertain the notion that Watanabe and I would become boyfriends, or even see each other again. I am sure he was equally clear about this. We "passionated" in the present, with no thought of the future. Because we were *completely* and *mindfully* involved in our present pursuit, there was a Buddhist spiritual element to our lovemaking.[3]

The memory of my first sexual encounter in Japan is etched in my heart. It was affectionate, even loving, motivated solely by lust. With our bodies, we transcended cultural, linguistic, and ethnic barriers.

Watanabe was not a hustler. As a matter of fact, I have been with only one hustler on my three visits to Japan. But the same kind of lustful yet meaningful encounter *is* available from hustlers and models. For the rest of this chapter I will be comparing cruising for casual sex with the utilization of hustlers' and models' services.

* * *

Of the various cruising venues, I am most familiar and comfortable with personal ads. I have written personal ads and responses to such ads, for myself, and for many friends and hustlers, going back to Toronto in 1963. I once taught a course on writing and responding to personal ads. All of my students were straight. Their experiences with ads were similar to those of gays.

Until fairly recently, a personal ad listed an address where respondents could get in touch with the advertiser. Most of the time respondents gave their phone number in the introductory letter, and things picked up from there. (The ones who did not give their phone number usually turned out to be frivolous.) Nowadays, personal ads are a big business for many newspapers and magazines. Advertisers generally can place ads free of charge, and respondents must use a 900 toll number to get in touch with them.

The written word is much more powerful than the spoken one. The advertisements as well as the letters of response are taken very seriously. A lot of thought goes into the phrasing of a brief ad (long ads are very expensive), and a lot of energy is expended on answering an ad. Also, an awful lot of money is spent on the toll calls. The publications where the ads appear make sure that even the briefest of messages will run into costly minutes!

When so much energy is expended on writing or answering an ad, one takes it for granted that the ad itself, and the correspondence it generates, will be read, ideally with great care, by all parties. This is often not the case at all. For instance, a friend of mine was an innovative ad writer, who placed ads in various gay publications on a regular basis. One day he asked me to drive him to pick up the responses, which were held for him at the publication. That particular ad elicited sixty-two replies. He was told that it was the most any ad had garnered in one week. I wondered how he would handle such an enormous volume. A few weeks later I asked him about it. "Oh, I just tossed all of them."

"Why did you do that?"

"I didn't feel like dealing with them."

The bunch of letters he tossed represented some one hundred hours of wasted energy by the sixty-two respondents. (Over the years, I have found out that throwing away replies is not all that uncommon.) It also left questions marks in the minds of the respondents. *Was my phrasing at fault? Did I write too little or too much? Should I really have written that I was not well hung but always got compliments on my screwing? Would he have answered my ad had I not mentioned that I was HIV positive?* They will never know the answers, and will have to agonize again over the same questions when answering the next ad.

Many advertisers and respondents are complete flakes. Men who want nothing more than a roll in the hay will advertise under "relationships" and refer to themselves as monogamous types. Respondents who are wan and haggard will describe themselves as trim and fit. Men in their fifties will respond to an ad seeking "youthful." Many flakes consider the process of responding to ads an exercise in creative writing, and feel little obligation to deliver what they have so eloquently promised in their letters. This flakiness is even more noticeable on the Internet. However, the energy invested in composing the perfect ad for an electronic bulletin board, and an e-mail as a witty response, is probably less than for a publication.

In view of the above, why should anyone spend time, money, and energy on answering ads? As with bars and baths, the ads sometimes achieve results. I know three couples who met through ads and have lived together, more or less happily, for many years. I know a number of people who found permanent sex buddies through the ads. Like all other gay venues, personals cannot be dismissed as entirely ineffective.

Since I am comfortable with personals, I advertise constantly and, on very rare occasions, have done very well for myself. These days, I place my ads in semistraight publications. The bisexuals and straights who respond all claim to have young girlfriends and seek a much older man for gay sex. (I cannot explain this phenomenon, and have not seen much research into the subject.) A number of young, cute, and horny guys have made cameo appearances at my home. Nothing lasting has ever developed.

I can afford the expenditure of energy on this hobby. When it works, I have more sex and see fewer hustlers or models. When the cameo appearances stop, which is most of the time, I have models whom I genuinely like, and with whom I have excellent sex, waiting for my call. This allows me to have control over my sex life. If I had to depend solely on the results of the personal ads, I would live in a state of permanent anxiety.

* * *

I like the sexual openness of gay bathhouses. The many games that are played there are all meant to culminate in getting laid. Baths are egalitarian institutions. There, one's education, wisdom, character, and wealth count for nothing. A person's physical attributes, from the color of his hair, the girth of his waist, the size of his biceps, to the shape and length of his penis, are all that count.

In the thousands of hours I walked through the corridors of scores of bathhouses, like a nomad in the desert desperately seeking an oasis, I ranted against cruel fate. By baths standards, I have never cut a popular figure. In the presence of beautiful queens and magnificent hunks, I have always felt like an insignificant supplicant, waiting to be recognized. That I have been chosen at all at baths in Honolulu, Vancouver, San Francisco, Mazatlan, San Juan, Amsterdam, Zurich, Munich, Barcelona, Tokyo, Manila, and many points in between is a testimony to my stubborn perseverance in the face of indifference and rejection. If I had to rely on the baths as a permanent sexual outlet, I would have thrown in the towel long ago.

Time in baths also counts for nothing. Most establishments will let you stay eight hours, and quite a few patrons extend that period by paying again in order to find a partner. The night I met my future lover at the baths was very successful for me because, atypically, I scored three times. Still, I remember running into a friend there and complaining that I was wasting my time. I had already spent two hours trudging up and down stairs, seeking a sex partner.

The problem is not only my lack of patience. Since most of the time I do not do well in baths, the time waste cannot be justified. The ambiance at the baths borders on the hostile. As a rule, patrons who are not interested in you sexually are barely civil when they reject you. Even though they are at the baths to solicit sexual advances, *you* happen to be the last person on the face of the earth they want to be solicited by. At times, this message gets communicated with a hissing malice. Sometimes, management deliberately creates a stressful environment. For instance, in some baths, on Saturday nights music is played extremely loudly to discourage patrons from staying the entire night.

In its heyday, San Francisco had some very spectacular baths.[4] In the basement of the Ritch Street Baths, for instance, was a restaurant with good food, next to a large Jacuzzi. On that floor there was also a substantial gym, and for relaxation, a patron could watch tropical fish swimming in large aquariums. The first floor had lots of clean, private cubicles; the second floor, in addition to cubicles, featured elaborate mazes to have sex in, as well as a porno theater.

The baths present an artificial *Fantasy Island* environment, with no carryover into real life. Most of the time, the great sexual encounters in the baths do not continue on the outside. But all of these visits cost a fair amount of money and *enormous* chunks of time.

Sometimes I suspect that the bathhouse trysts are meant not to carry over into real life. For a while, at the Berkeley baths, I would meet a man, Nelson, who was always there on Thursday afternoons. I made it my business to try to be there on Thursdays to connect with him. When we did, we always had a terrific time. Like me, he drove all the way from San Francisco to the Berkeley baths. As a matter of fact, he lived almost within walking distance of me. "Why don't we meet in San Francisco and save both of us the time and money?" I asked him once.

"I told you, I have a lover."

"But we're getting it on here on a regular basis, so why not at my place in San Francisco? What is the difference?"

He refused to meet me anywhere other than the baths. By a tacit convention, the baths are usually emotionally sterile. The sexual bonding that takes place there dissolves upon departure. This is an emotionally safe space to cheat on your lover.

To meet Nelson, I went to the baths on Thursdays. When that was over, I went to the same baths at the same time but on different week days. I spotted quite a few of the men I had seen on my Thursdays with Nelson. For all I know, they spent each afternoon of the week at the bathhouse searching for sex partners.

For many years, I forced myself to go to the baths. I did not have much money to spend on hustlers. Also, I was (to a certain extent I still am) brainwashed by gay society. I thought that it was better psychologically if I did not pay for sex, even if I had the money to do so, and even if the sex at the baths was markedly inferior to what hustlers could offer me.

Ultimately, it boils down to managing the scarcest resource we possess: time. For me, cruising time at the baths is a complete and unjustifiable waste. All the more so because it does not guarantee that there will be any compensation, that is, that I will find a suitable partner. It is also psychologically damaging to expose oneself deliberately to negative energy in the form of repeated rejections, a topic I will discuss later in this chapter. A good hustler can give me the same, or much better, sexual satisfaction. In the process of being with a hustler, I do not spend precious time frustrating myself. The time is spent on lovemaking. To me money is cheaper than time.

* * *

I have been told by many bar mavens that San Francisco's bars are notorious for the "attitude" of the patrons. With my limited bar experience, I, too, have noticed that gay bars outside my city tend to be friendlier. My bar observations, based on my San Francisco experience, are probably the worst-case scenario.

Bars have some advantages over baths. Men who go to baths do it for sexual, not social, reasons. If they do not connect sexually at the baths they have a negative experience. Bar-going is an acceptable *social* activity. Not picking up anybody at a bar does not mean that the visit was a total failure. People who live in dingy apartments or with too many roommates can, for the price of a drink, be in more congenial surroundings. Although bars, at least in San Francisco, can be as hostile cruising grounds as the baths, a regular at a bar is bound to meet some buddies there and won't feel as forlorn as at the baths. Bars are also a much more fertile ground for starting a dating relationship.

For a variety of reasons, in terms of wasting time and money, bars are much worse than baths. In the latter, if you are patient enough, *something* is bound to happen. In the bars, after many hours of drinking (an expensive and unhealthy pursuit) nothing might happen.

I know, I know, some readers will complain about me, "This author has nothing but sex on his mind. Normal people go to bars to drink, dance, chat with friends, and relax." Good for them. They are doing great, and should continue to frequent the bars of their choice. I happen to know a lot of gays—some of whom were my clients when I worked as a hypnotherapist—who go to bars to cruise, even though they loathe the loud music and the smoke. To be successful in their cruising, they need to drink heavily. In the end, they may waste a lot of time and money, flirt with alcoholism, experience rejections and frustration, and leave the bar without a date.

I prefer to meet my friends for cappuccinos in a café at 1 p.m., rather than for martinis in a bar at 1 a.m. If I go to bars at all, I would like to go to places where I can pick up suitable partners. Makes sense? Apparently not . . .

In the 1960s I found a bar I liked: Bligh's Bounty. As far as I know, it was the first bar in San Francisco to feature go-go dancers. It was racially completely integrated. For a wonder, I was popular there. Every other time or so, I would manage to pick up a go-go dancer and take him home. This impressed me so much that I shared the news of my good fortune with friends and acquaintances. My friends, aware of my sexual predilections, shrugged it off. My acquaintances were horrified. I was told it was a low-class bar catering to the worst elements. They urged me to go to bars where I would rub elbows with gays who were on the "A" list. In my naiveté, I thought that one went to bars where one could find eager partners. When it comes to bars I can't win for losin'.

Bars, much more than baths, interfere with keeping normal hours. Even if you stay late at the baths, when you leave you go home to sleep and prepare for the next day. If you leave with your beloved-for-the-night after the bars close, it is the *beginning* of a very busy time.

* * *

Over the years, I have heard many models tell the "Crumpled Bills" tale. In slightly different versions, the story goes likes this: A young, good-looking guy—as young and good looking as the model himself—shyly arrives for his first appointment. He is a novice. The model is turned on to this client, and they have a marvelous session. The model wonders to himself why this client would want to pay for sex since there is no doubt that he could get it for free. But, of course, the model never asks the question. At the end of the session, the client pays the model with crumpled one-dollar and five-dollar bills that he must have stashed away, one at a time, for days or weeks. I always believed this was an old models' tale. Then Jacinto told me the same story, showing me the crumpled bills!

A young, inexperienced man, who is not even sure whether he is gay, may solve the awkwardness of his first homosexual encounter by hiring and paying a professional with his hard-earned money. It is the only practical way to maintain a fair amount of control during initiation into gay sex. Once a young person starts using the services of hustlers by choice, not necessity, he will learn to appreciate them for the efficiency and the predictability they offer, as opposed to the vagaries of all other cruising venues. As a much older man, he won't feel that he must resort to hustlers because he is ugly and undesirable.

Later on, I will discuss extensively health and safety issues related to hustlers. For the moment, I want to emphasize the control the client, especially a novice, exercises in terms of what he wants or does not want done, such as be screwed in one specific position, using the condom and lubrication he provides, and, if he so desires, stopping the action in midscene. Inherently risky sexual behavior is also much safer with models. For instance, being tied up by a bondage aficionado, who may be carried away and not respect one's limits, is more dangerous than being tied up by a model who does it as a job and wants repeat business.[5]

Prostitution (the female variety) has been regarded by its opponents as threat to the stability of the family. Exactly the opposite is true. How many men would divorce their wives in order to marry prostitutes? Rather, the prostitute serves as a safety valve to let the husband "do his thing" and stay with his wife. Whether society, especially women, approves or disapproves of this safety valve is beside the point. The institution of prostitution has been in place for many thousands of years, and has probably saved many more marriages than it destroyed.[6]

It is similar with gay couples. Again, how many cases do you know of lovers splitting because one of them decides to make a sex worker his new partner? There is a pattern in the gay community of long-term lovers *not* having sex with each other. Their extramarital activities in baths and sex clubs are much more likely to dissolve the partnership with their lovers than are regular sessions with models. My trysts with Nelson at the baths presented a more serious threat to his relationship with his lover than having sex with a paid hustler. This is why he refused to see me at my home.

If I want to be on my best behavior on a first date, I will have sex with a hustler the day before the event. Hustlers help me control my libidinal drive when I want it to be on low.

* * *

Not everybody is able to deal constantly with rejections. Such people do not run for political office or become door-to-door salesmen. But rejections and cruising go hand in hand. The rejections are completely arbitrary, depending on the unique taste and the particular mood of the person being cruised. Occasionally, even the Great Hunks get rejected without knowing why their value plummeted suddenly on the Gay Exchange.

This brings me to my pet peeve: In spite of all the time I spent at the baths, I would be hard pressed to write a brief paper on successful cruising techniques there. What worked for me yesterday might not work tomorrow, and the man with whom I had hot sex a month ago may ignore my presence on my next visit. We rarely get verbal feedback from those who reject us, and so we do not know how we can improve ourselves. (This lack of feedback may also be true in other situations. But such situations do not arise ten times in one evening as they do at the baths!) The following is an anecdote to make my point.

In the wild 1970s in San Francisco, an enterprising man opened a gay bathhouse specializing in Caucasians who like Asians, sometimes referred to, pejoratively, as "rice queens." The business closed after a few months.

I went there during its first week. Not counting the staff, there were two other patrons in the bathhouse: a good-looking, young, uncommunicative Asian, and a Caucasian man. The latter was youthful, tall, and handsome, with a chiseled body. The three of us had arrived more or less at the same time. For a while, we sat in the main room, staring at each other, without exchanging a word. The Asian's expression was unfathomable. I had no idea whom he preferred. I suspected it was the man with the chiseled body. The latter stood up for a moment, and let the towel draped around his waist slip to the ground. Both the Asian and I beheld his manhood. A *very* impressive sight, indeed!

As a primate, I am genetically programmed to yield to the alpha male, or to challenge him and fight to the death. This was a no-contest. My rival was a magnificent alpha specimen. Compared to him I was a . . . never mind. I went to the corner of the room and cowered. I waited for the alpha to drag the Asian to his lair and mate with him there. But the impassive Asian did not react to the display of the alpha's manhood.

The tension in the main room was too much for me to bear. I went to the hall pretending to make the rounds, even though I knew there were no other patrons at the bathhouse. The Asian guy must have followed me. All of a sudden, I saw him standing quite close to me. He took my hand into his and led me to his room. His name was Tora. We had a good time with each other. I found out that he was from Japan, studying English here.

When we finished, and I had nothing to lose, I asked Tora why he preferred me to the alpha. "Oh, he is a *climinar*." It took me a while to figure out what Tora wanted to say. When I finally understood that he had meant "criminal," I was baffled. How did he know the alpha was a criminal?

It turned out that my rival had a tattoo on his upper arm. It must have been a small one, because I had not noticed it. In Japan, only members of the *yakuza* (the Japanese Mafia) have tattoos. Between a criminal alpha and a very ordinary gay man, Tora chose the latter.

By the time we finished, my chiseled-body rival had left. To this day, he must wonder why he did not win the contest. With his equipment, he was entitled to expect better. In desperation, he may even have added another tattoo to make sure that next time around Tora would not reject him.

Hustlers and models provide a welcome respite from rejection. It is the one venue in gay life where you are accepted the way you are (provided, of course, you have the wherewithal).

* * *

When I came to San Francisco and started playing for real, a set of new phenomena entered my life. I got stood up constantly by dates; many of the dates who did show up were very tardy; people I met and had good sex with gave me phony telephone numbers. These were brand new social situations that I handled poorly. I found out from friends that being stood up or given the wrong phone number by someone with whom you have had a hot sexual session was a regular occurrence. Over the years, I have discovered some coping mechanisms. But it still hurts a lot, and it still drains energy.

Many hustlers are lax about keeping appointments[7]—a subject I have already discussed. Models and masseurs, as a rule, are punctual, because it suits their own needs perfectly. I have noticed that when hustlers upgrade themselves to models (as distinguished from models who have never hustled) they tend to continue being flaky about appointments.

On my last trip to San Juan, Puerto Rico, I was stood up twice. Once, it was by a fellow hotel guest with whom I had had a fling, and whom I had invited for dinner. It ruined my evening because I could not replace him, on the spur of the moment, with another dinner companion. The second time, I was stood up by a hustler whom I had seen a number of times on my previous visit. I liked him a lot, and was sorry that he did not show up. After thirty minutes of waiting, I went downstairs and, in front of the hotel, picked up another hustler.

* * *

Hustlers and models are a hedge against the unpredictable results of cruising. I am not suggesting closing down the bars, bathhouses, and sex clubs, and training a cadre of a hundred thousand hustlers as substitutes. Rather, I advocate experiencing the luxury, once a week, a month, a year, of having a predictable, good sexual encounter with a hustler or model of your choice; using the services of hustlers when time is more important than money, or when you want sex without the hassle of cruising.

The results of cruising are not only kaleidoscopic. They are also Kafkaesque, that is, the rules of the game change constantly, but the players are not made aware of these changes. The chiseled-body alpha might well have felt depressed for a whole month having lost out to an omega in the mating game. Cruising brings with it manic-depressive mood swings—one moment we soar with the eagles, the next we are in the pits of despair. Hustlers and models are a good remedy to control such mood swings.

Chapter 8

Merchandising Lustful Energy

One cannot buy love. It has to be earned. But one can buy lustful sexual energy. This is the subject of this chapter.

Let me start with the story of model Peter. He advertised himself as "the boy next door." This description was especially accurate in my case, since he lived just over a block away from me. In the early 1980s I saw him four or five times.

When I made my first appointment with him, he asked me a lot of detailed questions about my sexual likes and dislikes—more technical questions than I had ever been asked on the phone. Just before hanging up he said, "Sometimes I am a little wild. So don't be surprised!"

As I walked one block downhill to his flat, I wondered what he had meant when he said that he was a bit wild. I soon found out.

When Peter opened the door, I saw before me a Chicano in his middle twenties. He had told me that he was "an average-looking guy." That was a factual description. There was nothing special or disproportionate about him. He really did look like a regular gay Hispanic guy next door. I liked the mischievous sparkle in his brown eyes, and his trim body.

I wish there had been a camera to film us in action. A jury would have been hard pressed to determine whether Peter date raped me or whether we had consensual, if somewhat violent, sex. From the moment I entered his apartment, Peter used just a little physical force to "persuade" me. He pushed me onto his bed and started removing my clothes, almost, but not quite, tearing off buttons. He staged it so well that I started resisting him, even while cooperating in the "rape."

Once we were naked, he "forced" himself on me vehemently. He acted so authentically that I rose to the occasion and whimpered,

"No" while cooperating with him. Since he had found out beforehand what I liked, the scene never went beyond my own limits. Peter expended so much energy that he was sweating heavily a few minutes into the scene even though it was one of San Francisco's foggy and cool summer afternoons. He climaxed just a few seconds before me. After I came, I could feel the beat of his heart. It was frighteningly fast. We hardly talked to each other. For Peter I was nothing but a sex object. The illusion that I was there solely for *his* pleasure faded away only when I paid him for the session.

What Peter did was to interpret the role of a model the way an actor interprets his assigned character. Peter's interpretation was unusual (he probably learned it from porno video) and was much more dramatic and effective the first time around than on subsequent visits.

Not only was Peter's interpretation unusual, he also expended more energy than most models. His excitement was real: his orgasm was not phony, and his rapid heartbeat was not fake. What I bought from Peter was lustful energy, which he delivered in great abundance.

But how could Peter turn on this energy at will? What happened when a client turned Peter off? For all I know, I might have turned him off. I had known the answer to this question for a long time from conversations with many hustlers but, still, I wanted to find out for myself.

Since I was too old to hustle on the street, I decided to do a simulation of this experience. I experimented half a dozen times, but will report here on the most successful event.

I used the Berkeley bathhouse as my lab, trying to duplicate the experience hustlers have when they are picked up by men for whom they may not care sexually, or who may even repulse them. Since the bathhouse in Berkeley presently accommodates patrons that used to be taken care of in many now-closed baths, the clientele there consists of a wide variety of people in terms of age, ethnic group, and body type.[1] It mirrors, more or less accurately, a random group of clients that a hustler on the street would encounter.

Field conditions are always different from a lab setting. For instance, it was impossible for me to duplicate the potential danger a hustler faces in a stranger's home, and the feelings this would evoke. A bathhouse is the safest place for sex with strangers, since the tiny, lockable cubicles provide only an *illusion* of privacy. The partitions are so thin that even whispers can be heard in the adjacent cubicles.

There was another problem with the baths. I wanted to make sure that I would not, through body language, make myself available to someone *I* chose. I wanted to be picked up by someone who fancied me, regardless of how I felt about him. My first experiment had to be aborted. No sooner did I make myself available to anyone, then I was chosen by the one guy who, under ordinary circumstances, would have been *my* favorite. Of course, under ordinary circumstances, he would not have looked at me twice!

This time I stood in the hallway looking neutrally at anyone who came by. At the baths, my look would be interpreted as *maybe he is interested in me.* It took only a few minutes before an old guy stood next to me, looking at me inquiringly. I smiled pleasantly, as his hand brushed against the towel draped around my waist. This man, physically very much an older version of myself, would make a good guinea pig, I thought. I had absolutely no sexual interest in him.

"Would you come to my room?" he asked.

"Yes."

Once in his cubicle, we sat on the bed. He embraced me and said: "You're the noblest person here today."

Noblest? In all my years at the baths, the most I was ever called was a lukewarm "cute," and that happened on very rare occasions. I was pleased.

We exchanged names. He put his arm around my shoulders and asked, "What do you like to do?"

Borrowing a line from Maestro Jed, I said, "I'm into pleasing."

Whereupon Jack French-kissed me. For a split second, I felt violated. I did not expect this old man to become so intimate with me. Then I remembered that I was into pleasing. I returned the thrust of his tongue enthusiastically. Soon our bodies were entwined and we were making out wildly.

I was becoming aware that I was physically sexually aroused. I say "physically," because mentally I was observing the experiment dispassionately, and was not the least bit turned on by Jack. It was the arousal gauge that signaled to my brain that there was more than an experiment happening. Aware of my arousal, I grew more passionate, to which Jack responded ardently.

During a break in our lovemaking I asked Jack how old he was. "I am seventy-four years old," he said. Seventy-four! The oldest person I had ever been with. There had not been too many guys half Jack's age with whom I had made out. "I am married, you know," Jack added.

"Are you bi, then?"

"Nah, I am really gay. I haven't had sex with my wife for many years. I told her that I was too old to fool around. When I go to the baths, I tell my old lady that it is a volunteer job. I haven't been screwed in many years. Would you like to do it to me?"

The last thing in the world I wanted to do was to screw Jack. But if the role required it, I was ready. "I suppose so," I said. "But only with a condom."

Jack thought it over for a while and, fortunately, gave up on the idea.

Then I made a mistake. I came before him. I'll write later about the problems of hustlers climaxing during a session. I felt as if a switch had been thrown. The lustful energy had been cut off. It became very difficult for me to continue our lovemaking. Experience took over. Hurriedly, I made Jack climax. He had not noticed my sudden lack of ardor. "I haven't had good sex like this in a long time. This was wonderful. Really wonderful," he said.

I was very satisfied with my experiment. Almost until the end, things went really well. To give the experiment the final touch of authenticity I almost asked, "Where is the green?" Very low-class street hustlers will tell their clients, before sex, "Show me the green." As we parted, Jack kissed me passionately, and both of us went to the showers.

The final chapter of this experiment was written a month later. I was at the baths again and ran into Jack. Seeing his "noble friend," he wanted an encore to the wonderful experience. I was not in my hustler mode. There was absolutely no way I could have had sex with Jack. I declined curtly, and moved away from him.

Hustlers had been telling me for years that they needed to psych themselves into doing a good job with their clients. But before I come to this topic I want to comment on my own behavior with

Jack. True to bathhouse aberrations, on one occasion Jack discovers a perfect and cooperative sex partner. The latter apparently enjoys sex with him greatly. A month later, the same noble sex partner will not even speak to him. Of course, Jack blames himself for his former sex partner's rejection. He must have offended his noble friend somehow. How could he possibly know that his partner was playing mind games when they had sex?

* * *

The first hustler who told me about psyching himself into sex was Alfonso, about whom I wrote in Chapter 4. Routinely, he would take out calls very late at night. For such calls he got paid very handsomely. "If I know the client, I don't mind getting up, driving over, and having sex with him," Alfonso told me.

"What difference does it make whether or not you know the client?" I asked.

"If I know him, I can psych myself into it."

In one way or another, hustlers use techniques that help them override their own physical preferences. One hustler told me that if he did not like a client, he would think about what he would do with the money he would get at the end of the session. Another concentrated on one physical trait he liked in the client, and managed to ignore the rest. David, a unique hustler, told me on the telephone when we set up a date, "I take only one client per day. For me it is a love sacrament." After a session with him, I knew he had told me the truth!

This ability to be professional in the face of unpleasant situations is not unique to hustlers. Lawyers defend criminals whom they abhor. They manage to ignore their own feelings, and put up a good defense for their clients. It is just our perception that sex workers are hypocritical when called upon to perform intimate physical functions that run contrary to their taste.

* * *

I managed to upset a number of people when I announced that I would write a book about hustlers, and gave them a preview of my project. One of them took the trouble to drop me a note, stating:

> What you pathetically describe as "relationships" with hustlers exist only by virtue of lubrication applied by you in order to get them to slip through your door for sex. Take away that lubrication, the sex and the so-called "relationship" would cease to exist.

This note was written by a retired social worker whom I consider a worldly man. Surely, he knows that however caring and dedicated a mental health professional is, once the "lubrication" is taken away, the treatment ceases. The same is true of all service providers. Had the writer of the letter viewed my relationships with hustlers as paid-for exchanges of lustful energy rather simulated love, he would not question their sincerity.

Contrary to what is implied in the letter, there is something essentially honest about hustling. The client buys a chunk of time from the hustler during which there is an exchange of lustful energy. At the end of the session, the hustler is paid for his time and energy. If any games are played, they take place during the stipulated time. Compare this to a sugar daddy relationship or, indeed, to all straight and gay marriages in which money plays a role!

As with any independent contractor, the professional association may lead to a social relationship. My friendship with some hustlers continued after I stopped being their client. Other hustlers, who were extremely competent and affectionate in bed, confined themselves to a professional relationship. Naturally, once I stopped being their client, we had no further interest in each other.

A good example of how straightforward hustling is compared to a sugar-daddy arrangement is the convoluted story of the late entertainer Liberace and his much younger "sugar son," Scott Thorson. When the very closeted Liberace wanted to get rid of him, Thorson was given $75,000 in exchange for waiving future claims. Eventually, Thorson sued Liberace for $113 million in palimony. This was thrown out by a Nevada judge as a "money for sex" arrangement. Even in Nevada, where prostitution is legal, this is unlawful.[2]

The letter and its reference to "lubrication" brings up the question of sincerity. Clients do not require hustlers to love them. But many clients require them to climax or, at least, have an erection during the session. There is no way that one can force oneself to "show a hard." When I was with Jack in the bathhouse I *was* physically aroused, in spite of being completely disinterested in Jack—or, at least, I believed this to be the case. This physical arousal, even though it was achieved through a mind game, started a flow of lustful energy.

Our professional personas always differ in various ways from who we really are. For most of my professional life, I taught children and adults. I have a vocation for teaching, though by nature I am a very impatient person. When working as a teacher, I have been quite successful in suppressing this trait. The suppression of my impatience for the sake of the profession does not make me a hypocrite.

A hustler is in the business of supplying lust. This is bothersome to many people because they are afraid to recognize lust as a benevolent energy, unrelated (though in some respects similar) to love. This energy can be bought, sold, and exchanged.

Lustful energy can even be generated and exchanged by persons who do not like, or even hate, each other. To illustrate: A few years ago, in answer to my ad seeking a steady (paid) sex partner, Woodrow, a twenty-one-year-old man, responded. He was the most intelligent sexual partner I had ever been with—by this I mean that he would have scored the highest on an IQ test. He had arrived from Taiwan some five years earlier, finished high school in the United States, and received a BS degree in chemical engineering at the age of twenty.

Upon graduating, Woodrow could not find a job in his field. Even the two menial jobs he had managed to secure did not last long. He blamed it all on his Chinese accent when he spoke English. This was nonsense. I knew Chinese with much thicker accents who had good jobs. I believe that it was Woodrow's personality that put off employers.

Woodrow was aloof, cold, argumentative, and, according to him, very awkward in social settings. His political views, which he liked to share, would have endeared him to the ultraconservatives, had they been open to embracing a Taiwanese immigrant. Except for his youthful appearance and sexual vigor, Woodrow was a crotchety old man.

According to Woodrow, I was only the third sexual partner in his life, and his first client. Physically, we were each other's type. Sexually, we were as compatible as can be, and fulfilled each other's expectations. The lustful energy flowed copiously between us.

Woodrow lived with his parents. His father, whom Woodrow thoroughly disliked, had been a high-ranking army officer in the Republic of China (Taiwanese) army. The last thing he would want was for his son to become a San Francisco queer. Woodrow was so closeted that we had to work out elaborate schemes to communicate with each other, until I convinced him to subscribe to a voice mail service.[3] That allowed Woodrow to work on his scheme of upgrading himself to a "sugar son." He was quite frank about his desire to live with an older—much older!—man, who would look after his needs. This would allow him to live away from his parents. I was his pilot project. Woodrow's quest for a real sugar daddy was as matter-of-fact as his plans for buying a car in the future. He was young, cute, and passionate, and there was a market for his services.

Though the physical attraction between Woodrow and myself never diminished, we genuinely disliked each other after a few sessions.

I make it a point to talk to hustlers about *their* interests. Woodrow was interested in social science. Here we clashed constantly. For instance, Woodrow thought that Singapore's autocratic government should be a role model for other countries, including the United States. It was impossible to dismiss Woodrow's opinions as uninformed or juvenile. He was especially well informed about current events, and his views were not immature. If anything, they were geriatric. Woodrow also expressed homophobic views, which did not sit well with me.

I do not know whether Woodrow had a calling for hustling, though I suspect he did. I was his sexual type, and *in bed,* we liked to do the same things. What puzzled me then, and still does, is that we could have been so very intimate (e.g., passionate kissing) in spite of our mutual antipathy.

I did not dismiss Woodrow because, at that particular time, nobody I knew could have pleased me sexually as much as he did. I am reasonably certain that *sexually* Woodrow felt the same about me. This type of arrangement could not have gone on forever, because the general antipathy would win over the sexual connectedness.

The matter was resolved by my four-week trip out of town. Woodrow found another, better-heeled client, and I was forced to seek a replacement. It took well over a year before I found someone with whom I was as compatible sexually as I had been with crotchety Woodrow.

I have written all of this to make the point that *lustful* energy is not *loving* energy. (Of course, it is much better for both parties if the lustful energy is exchanged between partners who like each other.) The hustler who provides the lustful energy is not expected to perform a bogus love ritual. Clients must not confuse the hustler's genuine lust with love.

* * *

As I have already discussed, hustlers do their work for many reasons. They overrule their own physical preferences to get it on with clients by using psychological tricks to psych themselves. But, in addition to mind games, there may also be another stimulus that facilitates their work.

When I had sex with Jack, pretending to myself that I was a hustler, I had decided beforehand that I would please *anyone* who wanted me to do so. I was willing to subjugate my own preferences to those of any sexual partner. Alas, I would have made a poor hustler. A month later, I could not repeat this act of subjugation.

I know for a fact that there are men who *enjoy* doing just that sort of thing on a regular basis. In the olden days at the baths—before AIDS—some guys would wait in the orgy room to be screwed by anybody who was so inclined; others would blow anyone who would allow them to do it. It was the complete lack of control and the indiscriminate sex that turned them on. For a hustler, having some desire to please all men with his body is a useful trait.[4]

This little sexual mind trip has no connection whatsoever to life outside the bed. The majority of hustlers are not particularly interested in pleasing others, including their clients, in a nonsexual context.

Chapter 9

Principles of Hustler Management

Originally, I was going to name this book *Principles of Hustler Management*. I did not do so because I did not want to give the impression of a strong client managing a weak hustler. I trust that by now the reader knows that hustlers and models are not inevitably weak vis-à-vis their clients. In any case, it is not about who the weaker party is. Rather, it is about how to conduct a relationship with an independent professional—always a complicated under-taking—and why, in the end, the client needs to take overall charge.

In general, the working relationship between clients and profes-sionals is more complex than that between employer and employee because it is much more ambiguous. For instance, even though the patient employs the physician, the latter usually is more powerful than the former. The client retains the lawyer, but it is the latter who usually dictates what the former should do.

Clients and their hustlers are in a similarly ambiguous relation-ship. It requires collaboration and coordination between both par-ties to have a successful sexual encounter. A client who tells the hustler, "I want you to screw me," bestows upon him enormous real and symbolic power. Even when the situation is reversed, most clients would want the hustler to be a cooperative and enthusiastic bottom, not a mannequin with an orifice.

Almost always, when the client interacts with the professional, the latter makes more of an impression on the former than vice versa. Your appendectomy scheduled for tomorrow at noon will be the only one in your entire life, but may be the fifth that day for the surgeon. Your investment in XYZ shares, recommended by your broker, may put at risk your life's savings, but is only one of scores of transactions that morning for him. You have fantasized for months about your 5 p.m. appointment with a model (which you can barely afford) but you are his second client of the day, and he has a dinner date with a prospective new boyfriend at 6:30 p.m.

In the end, the client who foots the bill can assert his ultimate power and withdraw further business from the professional. However, this does not make up for a lousy sex session with a model.

Given this ambiguous relationship between client and hustler, it is vital to achieve synergy between both parties. A client and his *regular* hustler (as opposed to a quickie pickup) define and redefine the working relationship between them constantly. There is no precedent to guide them, no script that they can follow.[1] Because the relationship is so amorphous one party needs to manage it, albeit by some form of agreement.

This and the following chapter are about creating a harmonious rather than adversarial relationship between clients and hustlers, under the management of the former.

* * *

Almost always, I have been very successful in my dealings with hustlers and models. My luck is due, in no small measure, to the fact that I started associating with them in my middle twenties. As a young man I felt fortunate that, accidentally, I had stumbled upon a practical solution to finding suitable sex partners when I needed and wanted them. Making my endless, mostly unproductive, rounds at the baths, I fantasized that one day I would be rich enough to engage hustlers 365 times a year!

As I grew older, I kept gaining more experience relating to hustlers (of late, mostly models), and my sex life improved with the years. When I listen to gay men many years my junior complaining how poorly they are doing sexually because of their age, I feel privileged that I regularly meet with the models of my choice, and have great sex with them.

My success with hustlers is also due to the fact that I enjoy being around them. Until a few years ago, I did not fully realize how much at home I was with hustlers. An incident in San Juan, Puerto Rico, opened my eyes. The gay hotel I used to stay at there is located in a cul-de-sac where many hustlers hang out day and night. I got to know most of them by name. The hustlers were a friendly and gabby bunch and I enjoyed talking to them. We had long conversations about this, that, and the other. I was challenged by the staccato Puerto Rican Spanish, which was quite difficult for me to follow. The hustlers were amused by my quaint, acquired Mexican Spanish, which sounded stilted to them. They were surprised that a much older hotel guest was interested in them in a nonsexual way.

One afternoon, I was shooting the breeze with a gaggle of them, and then walked into the hotel lobby to pick up my key. A fellow guest remarked contemptuously and loudly to the desk clerk, "Some guests at this hotel sure have weird friends." It was at that moment that I realized I was hanging out with the hustlers not merely to practice Puerto Rican Spanish, but because I genuinely liked my "weird friends." I found them much more interesting and colorful than the mainland moneyed elegant queens who were my fellow guests at the hotel.

My attitude toward hustlers and models has made it easy for me to create a *social* setting when we meet for sex. Some clients create an intense sexual ambiance for models. They offer alcohol, drugs, and porno to simultaneously relax and excite them. If host and model talk at all, it is, in the words of one hustler, about dick. Paradoxically, the charged atmosphere becomes intense and solemn rather than lighthearted.[2]

There is nothing wrong in creating such an atmosphere, but it makes sex the only item on the agenda. It allows for very little social talk before sex and, once sex is taken care of, the scene comes to an abrupt end and the parties go their separate ways. I have always tried to make my sexual encounters with hustlers into social occasions during which sex takes place. I believe that many hustlers prefer it this way. It must be very monotonous for them to talk about dick day in, day out. This does not mean the client is entitled to hog the hustler's time. Typically, these social occasions will become longer and more numerous as hustler and client get to know each other.

Chapter Nine of gay reporter Michelangelo Signorile's book *Life Outside* is titled "The Death of the Lonely Old Queen."[3] Signorile describes vividly the loneliness and self-loathing of some older gay men, versus the satisfaction of gay seniors who mentor the younger generation.

I did not start seeing hustlers in my twenties in order to become their mentor in my sixties. But it has worked out this way. Hustlers whom I see on a regular basis have often became my friends and protégés. (As is expected with people one cares about, I have also had lots of serious disagreements and fallings-out with some of them.) The secret has always been the sharing, to a limited extent, of our lives. Thus, there is one model in my life with whom I have sex a few times a year, but who comes by often to solve my computer problems. In return, I write his ads for him, since his English is shaky.

Every now and then, former hustlers drop by for social calls. I do not wonder whether I could have sex with them, and fantasize what sort of experience this would be. We already have had sex with each other! I do not have the gnawing sexual hunger of Signorile's Lonely Old Queen.

* * *

Full disclosure and ample communication are vital *before* bringing a hustler or model home or going to his place. Misstatements, by either party, are almost guaranteed to create unpleasant situations.

In Chapter 8, I wrote about my encounter with Peter, who all but date raped me. This was his little game. But, during our phone interview, he had gone out of his way to make sure that whatever he would do to me, once I came over, would be agreeable to me. He did not have real surprises for me, even though our entire encounter was a wild fantasy trip.

Similarly, while keeping up the illusion of spontaneity, the hustler should not be confronted by surprises such as the client demanding that he perform or acquiesce to acts that have not been contracted. In this respect, nothing should be left to the imagination, because understanding what and why hustlers do or refuse to do certain things is arcane stuff. Experience has taught me that hustlers view specific sex acts on three different levels.

The first level is how the world at large regards such sex acts. Screwing or being screwed are major events, compared to most other sexual activities. Obviously, a hustler must be told in advance that he will be asked to be a top or a bottom. He will feel entitled to charge his highest rate for "real sex."

The second level is how a hustler feels personally about certain sexual acts. I have run into quite a few hustlers who did not mind getting screwed but did not want to French kiss. This does not make much sense to me, but, since I like kissing more than screwing, I negotiate the kissing beforehand. I do not assume that because a hustler does not mind getting screwed he won't object to being kissed.

The third level is symbolic, that is, what the act represents to the hustler. Half the hustlers I know blow clients as a matter of course. The other half do not want to blow anyone except their boyfriends or significant others, or sometimes not anyone. On my birthday, one of my regular hustlers put a condom on me, and blew me for the first and only time, as a special treat.

A hustler told me the story of an angry client kicking him out in midscene. A few minutes after the hustler arrived at the client's home, the latter tenderly took off the hustler's shoes and socks and started licking his toes and feet. "Joseph," the hustler told me, "it tickled so much that it drove me crazy. I laughed and squirmed and the customer got real mad at me."

As he told me this, he started giggling hysterically, and then broke out into uncontrolled laughter. I could imagine how furious the client must have been. When someone laughs at your way of having sex, especially your favorite act, it deflates you completely. Had the client told the hustler beforehand, "I want to suck your toes," the hustler would probably have said, "OK, but I am ticklish. It will make me laugh." Both parties would have been forewarned, and it would probably not have become such a big issue.

A sex act that is easy enough for most healthy males to perform presents a possible complication for a hustler: climaxing for the benefit of the client. Here, again, what appears simple is, in practice, a complicated subject.

If it is essential to you that the hustler climax during the session, he should be informed and consent to it before you bring him home or go to his place. If this is optional, then the subject does not need to be brought up. But why on earth would the hustler *not* want to climax?

On the simplest level, a hustler may not want to climax because it will make it more difficult for him to turn another trick. His level of arousal may decline and he may not be able to maintain an erection. This varies from hustler to hustler. I have brought street hustlers home who ejaculated abundantly, of their own initiative, long before I did. When I brought them back to the street they stood at their former spot ready for the next client. Obviously, they could climax a few times in one evening. Others, of the same age group, apologized for not climaxing because they found it difficult to hustle after doing it.

Some hustlers find it difficult to climax because they are not aroused physically by the client and have problems getting an erection. Larry, a model I have seen off and on for some six years, rarely even gets a full erection. He is, however, one of the most affectionate kissers I have met. Though physically not very aroused, he has a good attitude: he wants to please the client and, without doubt, enjoys being affectionate. I have had enough experience to know that his affection is not faked. He climaxed with me only once as a symbolic act of gratitude for a favor I had done him.

Which brings me to the symbolism involved in ejaculation. Hustler Alfonso, about whom I wrote in Chapter 4, never climaxed with any client. Since most of his clients wanted to be screwed, he faked orgasms over and over again. (It helped that he was a drama major!) He took great pride in the fact that he *never* let his clients partake of his "essence." He told me that he would masturbate every morning to make sure that he would not accidentally climax with a client. On some symbolic level, in his own eyes, he was the winner. The clients paid him, but he did not *fully* repay them.

Then Alfonso went to Los Angeles for his junior year in college. He called me from there and asked me whether, during the winter break, he could stay with me. Before I could give him an answer, he said, "I'll pay you for your hospitality in my own way."

I was intrigued. Alfonso was not without friends. Why would he choose to stay with a client on his holidays?

It turned out that he wanted to do out calls with his former clients. For this he needed access to a phone (this took place before beepers) and to be able to speak openly. His friends did not know about his hustling.

He paid me by having sex with me four times in one week. On the first occasion he came in my mouth (that was before AIDS). "Was that an *accident?*" I asked him worriedly.

"No, that was my present for you for being a nice guy."

Of course, hustlers will, at times, do more than had been agreed upon originally, either because they feel like it in the heat of passion, or as a treat for a deserving client. But the move should come from the hustler, not the client. The agreement may be renegotiated by either party, for future sessions. It is a psychological error to put the hustler on the spot by asking him, "If I gave you another $30 would you . . . ?" He may acquiesce because he needs the money but will resent it later.

Should the client negotiate the length of the session in advance? I do not, though most clients do. Let's examine the issue from both sides.

The hustler/model sells lust for a given period of time. For additional periods of time he charges an additional fee. As far as he is concerned, the meter starts running when he reaches the client's home. If an hour has been agreed upon, then the drink he is offered and the chit-chat are part of the sixty-minute session.

From the client's point of view, the hour starts when there is an exchange of lust. If the client shows the hustler a porno video, that is done for the latter's titillation and should not start the meter.

It gets even more complicated. If the hustler stays the night—with an appropriate higher fee—how much sleeping time should he be given? Does the fee mean that the client is entitled to demand that his companion be awake the entire night for sexual exchanges and talk? The client may feel that at, say, $200, the hustler's time is all his. The latter may have to go to school or work the next morning and may feel that good sex before falling asleep and just "skin contact" for the entire night are worth the $200.

By convention (really, the *only* convention), when the client climaxes the session is over. Suppose you stipulated with the hustler that he would spend an hour with you. Somehow, you did not pace yourself properly and climaxed after ten minutes. Is the hustler supposed to stay another fifty minutes? If he wants to take a shower before he leaves, is this part of the fifty minutes?

To avoid all of this, I leave the subject open and try to concentrate on quality time, being mindful that I hired the hustler for a reasonable period of time. If the length of the session has not been stipulated beforehand, the hustler is not as tempted to check his watch constantly and see how much time is left.

Once a hustler becomes a regular, a routine is established. I have no problem with a hustler I see often who says to me, "Tuesday afternoon it will have to be a quickie, because I have a class at 6 p.m." I know that next time we will spend a lot of time together.

I think it is unprofessional on the part of the hustler, on the phone, to ask the client personal questions unrelated to the sex act, such as, "How much do you weigh? How old are you?" But, when this happens, full disclosure on the part of the client is essential. For instance, if a masseur does not want to exert himself working on an obese man—a very unprofessional attitude—then it makes no sense, for the client's sake, to give erroneous information about his weight.

Speaking of masseurs, if you want to be "released" it is *essential* that you ask on the phone whether the masseur offers a "full-body" or a "release massage." If you want to do more than be massaged (e.g., blow the masseur a bit) you must agree on it in your telephone conversation. If the masseur's answer is vague, such as, "You'll get a good massage and we'll see how it plays out," you may, rarely, get much more than just release, or, more likely, no release at all.

* * *

In my many years as a patron of hustlers, I have never been able to afford the asking price of San Francisco hustlers, because I saw them regularly rather than occasionally. Even when I used to go to the baths routinely, I saw hustlers on a regular basis, unless I was dating at the time. (I never had the psychological stamina to go to the baths twice in a row!) I have always had to negotiate fees that would fit into my limited budget.

In Chapter 1 I related how I first got the idea of setting up a hustler budget. This budget grows or shrinks depending on my financial circumstances, and has to be adjusted for inflation. (In the winter of 1965, I paid my first San Francisco regular $7 per session. In 1997, I paid my regulars $50.[4])

I have traveled a lot in third world countries. Hustlers there charged so little (when converted to U.S. dollars) that I could actually pay them more than they asked for.[5] To my surprise, in such countries I often found a single traveling companion, and took care of all his financial needs while we were together, plus a monetary gift when we parted.[6] Maybe there was not enough challenge in playing the rich tourist, picking up hustlers wherever and whenever I desired.

Back to San Francisco. Hustlers are not MDs or lawyers whose charges must not be challenged because of their august professional standing. I do not wish to discuss here the pricing policies of physicians and attorneys except for one observation: members of these professions study very hard and for many years before they are allowed to establish a practice. All hustlers need to do to become sex workers is to hang out on an appropriate street corner, or insert an ad in a gay paper! A prospective client need not feel any qualms about making a counteroffer to a hustler's asking price.

Negotiating an appropriate compensation for a street hustler is somewhat different than for a model. Hustlers have a more difficult time understanding that you do have the cash for their asking price but are unwilling to fork it over. With them, it makes sense if you say something they can relate to, such as, "Today is the thirteenth of the month. I don't get paid until the fifteenth. I can't give you the $80 you are asking for because I need some spending money for the next two days. Could we do it for $60?"

Models who, themselves, have bills to pay are financially more sophisticated than street hustlers. They understand that even though you have $100 to your name, you would be unwilling to spend it all on them because you have other financial obligations.

When no price is mentioned in a model's ad the question of his fee will come up during the phone conversation. He might say, "I charge $100."

"For an in or an out call?" the client may ask. (In calls are supposed to be less expensive than out calls.)

"I make only out calls."

"One hundred is more than I can pay. If we did it during the day, when you probably don't have many clients, would it be possible for you to adjust the price?" There needs to be some way for the model to come down in price with dignity. If you work days, you can ask,

"How about Saturday morning?" The reaction of the model will depend, first, on how much business he has and, second, whether he feels comfortable with you and your sexual scene. Once you become a model's regular, additional special arrangements can be made.

From handling Jacinto's calls, I learned how the fee can be negotiated even if it is stated in the ad. (The whole purpose of stating the fee in the ad is *not* to have to discuss it during the phone interview.) Jacinto advertised that he charged $50 for a massage. A few callers inquired whether he would charge them only $40 for a forty-five-minute massage. He always accommodated them because he needed the income. I spoke to one forty-dollar client. He *grossed* $11.50 an hour. Jacinto *netted* $50 for the same period of time. The client would have had to work the better part of a day to be touched by Jacinto's magic fingers! No wonder he wanted to pay less than the stated fee.

* * *

Most important for all hustlers and models is that the client not give them a hard time. This is not so much related to what the client does or wants done, but how he goes about it. (After the first meeting the hustler knows whether he can handle the physical part of the assignment.) A hustler told me about a favorite client of his who is into infantilism, which involves changing the client's wet diaper, feeding him baby food, playing baby-mind games, and so on. Since his client goes about it in a good-hearted and natural way the hustler does not mind, in spite of the messiness. The same hustler complained about another client who pays well for late night calls, but irks him with his maudlin drunken demands that next time around they have sex for free.

After a few excellent sexual sessions, preceded or followed by a pleasant conversation, there is a temptation to "normalize" the relationship between client and hustler, that is, do without the money exchange. The client's rationale is that the hustler *obviously* enjoys the encounter just as much as he himself, so why pay the former? Dispensing with the money part becomes even more tempting if the client goes out of his way to do the hustler special favors.[7] Do not succumb to this temptation because you will be disappointed in the hustler's totally negative reaction.

Hustlers run a business. The good session and pleasant conversation do not change the business arrangement—it just makes it more enjoyable for both parties. I am sure that had I connected with Maestro Jed at a bathhouse and persisted in chasing him, we would have had free sex with each other once or twice a year—when Jed was horny enough, the time was convenient for him, and if, miraculously, he still had my phone number. Jed got paid for being available to me when I was horny, and when it was convenient for me. Without the monetary inducement, Jed would have preferred watching TV while doing drugs.

* * *

As I have already written, the answering machine has made it possible for models to run their businesses efficiently out of their homes. Until recently, they had to take care of calls from legitimate clients, as well as contending with callers who literally made jerk-off calls or, worse, harassed them. The harassment consisted of verbal abuse and of making phony appointments. (Worst-case scenario: making an appointment for an out call and giving the model a nonexistent address.) To protect themselves against the latter, models tried to call back a prospective client to verify his number. I write "tried," because some callers do not keep appointments even if the models have their correct home phone numbers. (What are models going to do with the jerk's phone number? Report him to whom?)

Now a majority of hustlers use beepers without a voice mail capability. This frequently results in a nifty game of phone tag, in which the parties never connect or, if they do, it is too late for making appointments.

Many models deliberately ignore beeps when they cannot take on assignments. Most of their callers want action *now*. If the models are too busy that day, they do not bother to call back just to talk to a prospective client. Dealing with beepers can become very frustrating, and requires a special technique to get satisfactory results.

The late afternoon seems the best time to beep most models, since many of them work during the day. (Some will answer the beep from work but cannot talk freely.) Of course, if you manage to catch a model who does not work, the earlier in the day the better. If he is free, he might give you a good deal because this is his slow time. You might also consider making an appointment for the following day, which gives both parties more flexibility.

So, in the late afternoon, you look at the gay paper. You check the ads that appeal to you, ranking them from lowest to highest. You call the highest-ranking ad first. If all you can do is punch in your number (sometimes the beeper will have a voice mail option), write down the phone number you called, and a brief summary of the ad. Unfortunately, many models with beepers do not mention a name in their ads. The only way you can identify them when they call back is by their phone number.

You wait fifteen minutes and, if you receive no return call, go to the second ad on the list, repeating this process as many times as necessary, until you make contact and set up an appointment with a suitable model. I ask models who call after an appointment has already been made with someone else to give me information about themselves for a future meeting.

Beeping models and then having to wait for them to call back is tedious. I do it very rarely, only when all my backup systems are down. *Simply not having to deal with this chore makes seeing regulars a preferred option.*

With my regulars, I make my appointments days ahead of time. I am often asked how I know that I will be horny next Wednesday at 7 p.m. The person who asks me this question will also be the one who invites me for a special dinner two months in advance. How do I know that I will want to have dinner then? If I am in good health, I will be in a mood to have sex three days hence and dinner two months down the road.

The best thing about seeing hustlers and models is that clients do not need to impress them sexually or, indeed, in any other way. I have experienced very few performance failures with hustlers, and these were invariably due to drugs prescribed for some physical ailment. On those rare occasions, I did not lose the hustler because I could not climax. Rather, he comforted me and told me that on our next date things would work out. He did not want to lose me.

In the next chapter, I will write about how I managed one hustler over a period of many years. I will discuss useful and practical management strategies. Why manage hustlers at all? Why not see different hustlers for variety, and not have to deal with any managerial problems?

There are many reasons for sticking with fewer hustlers and models. Sex becomes better once the participants are used to each other; it is tiring and boring to find new hustlers all the time; it is safer all around to limit one's exposure to fewer hustlers.

I have always had to make special financial arrangements with hustlers and models to get a quantity discount as a regular. Naturally, as I get to know them, I start socializing with them. This makes the experience more meaningful. Of course, not all hustlers and models are open to more than a sex session. I do not become their regular.

Clients who limit their contacts with hustlers and models to sex shortchange themselves. A regular hustler is a *paid* sex buddy. Of course, one can meet a sex buddy on a regular basis without taking a personal interest in him, but after a few times this become old hat. (My encounter with Watanabe in Tokyo was great fun because we did not understand each other and had to rely only on body language. After ten times, the lack of communication would have become tedious.)

I have been asked many times how I find subjects of common interest with hustlers, as if they were somehow different from other gay pickups. I relate to them the same way I relate to people in general. Hustlers who are often (not always) younger and poorer than their clients are gratified when they are asked about their lives and their issues, and are taken seriously.

Some eight years ago, I met Darell, a Polk Street hustler. For a while, we saw each other on a regular basis. One day I had a splinter in the thumb of my right hand and could not get it out. When I brought Darell home I asked him, "Can you help me get the splinter out of my finger?"

"I'll try," he answered.

I handed him a sterilized sewing needle to help him dig it out. This is how I learned to do it when I was a child. "Man, that's not the way you do it."

"How do you do it, then?"

"Do you have nail clippers?"

"I do. But I have never heard of it being done this way."

"Well, that's the way I do it."

"Whatever works is fine with me," I said. I brought him the nail clippers. "Here you are. Please perform the procedure."

A moment later the splinter was out. "Well, Darell, thank you. I learned something new today."

"I'll say one thing for you, Joseph. You do listen to people."

Had Darell verbalized his entire train of thought it would be something like, "Joseph, you are one smart dude who does listen to people, even if they are hustlers, *and* young, *and* black."

That day I earned Darell's respect. Not many clients did!

Some clients try to impress their hustlers with, of all things, their riches. No person in his right mind would tell a plumber or an auto mechanic that he was very rich. So why make a statement like this to a hustler?

Apparently, many clients compare themselves to their hustlers and find that they are wanting: the latter are younger, handsomer, slimmer, better hung, and more muscular. (These are precisely the attributes they are hired for!) These clients must feel that the only thing they have going for them is having more money—lots of it—than their hustlers. If you tell a hustler that you are very rich you invite gouging!

* * *

Just as a patient may fall into the hands of a poor dentist, a client may contract the services of an incompetent or incompatible model. Some clients are so traumatized by one bad experience that they give up hustlers and models altogether. Just as a patient must not give up on dentists because of one unfortunate incident, a client ought not to disavow hustlers because a few do not work out.

Sometimes it is possible to get out of a bad deal with only a minimal loss of money. (Before I write about this, a caveat: nobody ever looks exactly the way you visualized him during the phone interview. You need to make allowances for this fact.) If you arrive at a model's home and he does not turn you on, you can simply tell him that he does not look the way you imagined him, and just leave. Personally, I would be inclined to offer him some money if I felt that there was no chemistry between us, but not, if he had misrepresented himself. In either case, do not be rude to him.

It is more complicated when a model arrives at your place. Whether or not he misrepresented himself, dismiss him gently. You do not need a vengeful model who knows your home address in your life. You can give him the same line I mentioned in the preceding paragraph, plus some cash. It might even be a good idea to have this cash ready, to avoid having to ask him to make change from a large bill.

Once the sex act has commenced, he is entitled to his full fee, unless he does not perform the specific act for which he has been hired, for instance, he cannot screw you because he cannot get an erection. In this case, the deal can be renegotiated. Again, do so diplomatically.

Chapter 10

A Practicum

In this chapter I will recount the history of my relationship with one hustler over a period of six years. Many of the problems clients face when dealing with hustlers surfaced in this particular relationship. Describing it will serve as a case study for a long-term client-hustler relationship. I will digress whenever I feel that I need to elaborate on a relevant subject.

Off and on, for almost six years, I dealt with a hustler named Gabriel. This was not a minor achievement, since Gabriel considered it his karma to manage every man who was sexually attracted to him, of whom there were many.

Gabriel came into my life at the end of 1985, right after Jed. He was introduced to me by Paul, a mutual friend, who was about to leave San Francisco, and was worried about Gabriel's financial well-being. When we first met, Gabriel was twenty-five years old. He had already retired from an illustrious career as a hustler and sometime porno star, and upgraded himself to a position that he had created for himself. He had two gentleman who, in return for occasional sexual favors, took care of his rent, utilities, and phone bill. (Each gentleman was assigned specific expense items.)

Gabriel, a short-order cook, was both an alcoholic and a workaholic. He held a full-time job, and sometimes worked at additional part-time catering assignments. Most of his income went for alcohol, occasionally for drugs, but, principally, for very expensive clothing and jewelry.

I remember well our first meeting at a café. Gabriel was tall, very slim, with brown, dreamy, almond-shaped eyes flanked by long lashes, and thick, long black hair arranged into a braid. He was the son of a Chinese mother and an African-American father. His facial features were Asian; his skin color was African. I like exotic and cute. Gabriel was exotic, cute, and very handsome. Maybe pretty would be a better word, because he was rather effeminate. He radiated enormous sex appeal. When I got to know him better, I would think of him as a female insect emitting pheromones compelling males from far and wide to fly and mate with her. As I would discover later, even men who were into macho partners made an exception for the effeminate, pheromone-emitting Gabriel.

He was shy by nature and spoke elegantly, in a soft, subdued, cultured voice. He told me that he had a boyfriend in Germany, a high school teacher, and was saving money to go there and live with him. After some ten minutes of chit-chat, he gave me a coquettish look and asked, "So, do you like what you see?"

The boldness of his question took me by surprise. He appeared to be so shy. In time I would find out that beneath the shy facade dwelt an imperious queen. "You are very handsome; very much my type."

"I told you that I was trying to save money for my trip to Germany. What arrangements do you have in mind?"

I was not immune to Gabriel's pheromones. I had heard enough about him to know that whatever arrangements I made, they would have to be very simple and straightforward. Otherwise, things would get out of hand financially. A quid pro quo arrangement would be best. The last thing I wanted was to become Gabriel's suitor. For this I had neither the money nor the stamina to fight off all his other suitors.

"How much did Paul tell you about my economic circumstances?" I asked.

"He said that he did not think you were very wealthy, but that you owned your own home and paid guys for . . . doing it."

"Well, that's correct, Gabriel. Why don't we have a trial session? What fee did you have in mind?"

"Fifty dollars per . . . deed."

I thought "deed" was an elegant term for getting laid. "If you stood on Polk Street, Gabriel," I said, "you could ask and get $50. If you advertised as a model you could ask $70. In either case, you would probably also get a handsome tip. However, if we're compatible, I'll become a regular, and you won't need to waste your time or money to find other clients. How about $30? This is what I pay your colleagues."

He thought it over for a moment. "Paul told me that you did deeds with the same guys. I need a regular. Done deal."

Of course, we were compatible. Unlike Jed, Gabriel was not a casual hustler. He was a male courtesan schooled in the art of pleasuring clients. Earlier in his life, Gabriel had worked for agencies, had run his own ads, and had performed a few heavy S/M and other fantasy scenes. When Jed needed money, he would do a singing gig, turn a trick, bake bread, whatever. He was not dedicated to any particular way of making a living. Gabriel used his sexuality to bring in the hard cash to cover his enormous expenses.

After the first session, I started seeing Gabriel on a regular basis. Within a few months, with the exception of the baths and dating guys I met there, I had sex only with Gabriel.

He insisted that I pick him up from his home or from work, and drive him back after we "did the deed." My Achilles' heel in my dealing with hustlers has been the picking-up issue. I live on top of one of San Francisco's steep hills, in an area that is not served well by public transportation. Nevertheless, like most of my neighbors, I cope with these difficulties when I have to use public transportation to go downtown where parking is all but impossible. But, then, we are not hustlers!

Hustlers expect their clients to pick them up and return them to base, or pay cab fare. (Models without their own transportation will incorporate the cab expense into their fees.) A hustler who will commute to work for an hour by bus and streetcar nevertheless will insist that a client paying fifteen times his hourly wage also see to chauffeuring him to and fro.

I have employed more than one hustler to perform various jobs in my house. It has always been understood, without ever having been discussed, that if they performed an "ordinary" job for me, they would get to my place by taking public transportation. Only in their hustler capacity do they demand being chauffeured to and from their assignments.

It does not help that I am a compulsively punctual person and that many hustlers (not all) have problems with punctuality. Gabriel, for instance, had lost a number of jobs for being tardy. As with Jed, Gabriel and I had lots of fights over this issue. It was maddening for me to drive through rush-hour traffic, managing to be right on time in front of his own home, and then have to wait for him for ten minutes to come downstairs.

Just a year ago I finally solved the transportation problem. I pick up hustlers who do not have cars at a central Castro district location *after* they call me to tell me that they are there, waiting for me. This way, they have to wait the five minutes it takes me to drive there. This new arrangement works most of the time.

When I picked Gabriel up, he was almost always in a bad mood. He regularly fought with his co-workers and roommates, whom he referred to as "lowlifes." (Gabriel was a real snob. I suspect that this is the reason he gave up on public hustling.) Most of Gabriel's problems revolved around his inability to relate to other people, including the kind gentlemen who paid his bills. As a result, a gentleman assigned to a specific expense item would, in a fit of rage, resign his commission and plunge Gabriel into a financial crisis.

This is where I, with my paltry $30 per deed, came into the picture. I think that Paul had introduced us so I would provide a backup safety net, when the other ones failed.

When it came to money matters, Gabriel and I got along splendidly because our arrangement was straightforward. While I was flabbergasted by the magnitude of Gabriel's phone bills (some months close to $1,000), the gentleman who had to pay for them was furious. I was happy that I could remunerate Gabriel on a pay-as-you-go basis, rather than have nightmares about his next phone bill. It was, in fact, the cheapest way to have sex with Gabriel.

This "fee per deed" had one great advantage for Gabriel. The gentlemen who took care of Gabriel's expenses would be hit upon for loans that he never repaid. Eventually, they refused to lend him more money, which caused a lot of tension. In my case, Gabriel could borrow money from me without either of us worrying about repayment.

It worked very simply. He would borrow $100 which he would pay back in "deeds," in five installments of $20 each. I insisted that I pay him $10 per session. This arrangement allowed him to pay off his debt while still making some money every time we got together. These arrangements could become very complicated. I made sure that we kept books. As with other hustlers, I asked Gabriel to make the entries in his own handwriting. This way he knew that the information was accurate.

Nonitinerant hustlers are usually good credit risks, provided they are expected to pay off through sex sessions. I have been burned only once by a hustler. In one case, it took me a whole year to collect. The hustler had borrowed money from me and then, unexpectedly, left town. When he came back he called me and said that he wanted to repay his debt, and have me as a client again. While he did not have a cent to his name, he was able to discharge his debt and make some money in addition.[1]

Gabriel's bad humor could easily be mistaken for bitchiness. When I got to know him better I interpreted his moods as melancholy. He had had a very unhappy childhood. In spite of his vibrant sexuality and imperiousness, he was a very sad human being. Typical of my relationships with other hustlers, Gabriel's moods never once were reflected in the quality of his sexual performance. This is how you separate the sheep from the goats. Gabriel was a professional hustler, who provided services when the client wanted them, not when he was in the proper frame of mind.

After we became comfortable with each other, he often stayed at my place to watch TV because he did not have a set of his own (too practical an outlay for him, and too cumbersome to move when he fell out with the people he lived with!) and his roommates did not watch the programs he liked.

Clients often complain that hustlers do not spend enough time with them. On occasion, I have felt that hustlers spend too much time with me, or, conversely, that I waste too much time consorting with them. Since hustlers sell their time, they are unwilling, initially, to give the client a lot of time before or after the sex act itself. But it was in Gabriel's interest to spend time at my house. He had no friends at all, except for Wolfgang, the German schoolteacher to whom he talked endlessly on the phone. The various gentlemen who helped support him insisted on having sex with him every time he visited them. Gabriel wanted them to beg for it, and doled it out parsimoniously.

With me, each sex act was paid for regardless of whether he spent an hour or the whole night (which happened quite often).[2] Most important, we did not play games with each other. He offered superb sex and, as time progressed, a friendship of sorts developed between us. I became Gabriel's confidant and confessor. I grew to like him but his melancholy and alcoholism made socializing difficult. Curiously, even though Gabriel's assignment was to amuse and pleasure me, it always fell to me to cheer him up and comfort him.

Sometimes Gabriel worked a sixty-hour week. He saw me once or twice a week, and had to visit his two gentlemen with some regularity. In addition, he spent a considerable amount of time in bars, meeting sexual partners he fancied for one-night stands. Where did all this time and sexual energy come from?

The answer lay in Gabriel's sexual prowess. On one evening, after work, and interspersed with a lot of alcohol, he would have sex with me, later on with one of his gentlemen, and much later still pick up a one-night stand in a bar. I am certain that, sexually, he acquitted himself well with my successors. The next day he would go to work in a very foul mood, and pick a serious fight with a co-worker. He was fired, or forced to resign, from numerous jobs. But he was very good at what he did at work and, as a rule, had no major problems finding another job.

Life as a gay person would have been considerably easier for me had I developed a liking for alcohol. I would have been one of the boys. Unfortunately, it does absolutely nothing for me. I used to have a perfunctory drink when I went to gay bars as the price of admittance—before AIDS only alcoholics and patients recovering from hepatitis ordered soft drinks. At home, I would keep some beer and sherry for guests. I have never in my life even come close to getting drunk. My tolerance for happy drunks is minimal. It is zero for morose drunks. Gabriel fit into the latter category.

By rights, I should have withheld all alcohol from Gabriel. But nothing in life is black or white. When he was tipsy, Gabriel transformed himself from a professional hustler to an insatiable sex machine. At this stage, our sex ascended to a higher plane.

I tried limiting the number of beers he could drink by not having more than two on hand. This did not make him very happy with me. Since this also controlled the intensity of his sexual output, I was punishing myself.

Things finally came to a head. Gabriel wanted to watch a program on public television on a Saturday evening. I had an engagement at the same time. I told him that he could watch the program by himself and, when I came back, we would do a deed.

Since the deed was not the main event of the evening, Gabriel was gracious enough to take the bus, rather than have me pick him up. He arrived just before I left. He made a cup of tea for himself, and installed himself in front of the TV. By that time, I trusted Gabriel fully and had no qualms about leaving him by himself.

When I came back, Gabriel was lying stark naked on the floor of the living room. In front of him were arrayed five empty beer bottles. He was polishing off the sixth. On the floor was also an empty six-pack container. I wondered where all these bottles had come from, but was given little time to solve this puzzle. Gabriel was in heat and pounced on me.

That night he even performed the one sexual act he had reserved exclusively for Wolfgang—he started blowing me. Experience had taught me that when hustlers perform, or let the clients perform, a sexual act they reserve for a special person, they feel very guilty about something. In the midst of Gabriel's overwhelming passion, I wondered why he felt so guilty. I knew it was not because he had gotten drunk. So what could it be?

As he was blowing me—lucky Wolfgang!—the answer popped into my head. Gabriel had arrived at my home without beer and there was none in the house. He must have gone out to buy the booze. Since he did not have the keys to my house he must have left the door unlocked so he could get back in. This meant that he left the door unlocked to go shopping. This would have taken him some fifteen minutes!

I asked him about it. Disengaging my penis, he mumbled that I was right but he had been out only very briefly. I was very angry. I stopped his blowing and told him to get dressed. That sobered him up. It had probably never happened to him before that a client he blew stopped him in mid-act. "I am very disappointed in you and I want you to go home now."

"You mean we are not going to do a deed?"

"Correct."

"But I don't have any money."

"Tough."

"How the hell am I supposed to get home?"

I had to drive him home. In the car he alternated between maudlin and abusive, all the time trying to excite me sexually. When we reached his apartment house he asked, "When are you going to see me again?"

"I don't know. Maybe in a month."

"Do you know anyone who'll give you better sex?"

"No."

"Is there anyone who'll do it for less money?"

"No."

"So there," he said, as he got out of my car.

I had ignored completely my own hustler-management principles. I had known almost from the very beginning of my consorting with hustlers that I could not depend on one supplier. Not only because of the unreliability factor, but also because it would give the sole hustler a psychological advantage. With Gabriel, the situation was atypical. For one, though he was habitually late he never stood me up. For another, he was by far the best hustler I knew. And he was affordable.

All of these considerations did not justify having no backup system in place. I knew that Gabriel was going to Germany—it had just taken him a very long time to get organized—and a replacement would have to be found.

I did not see Gabriel for the next four months. My first visit to the baths after suspending Gabriel bore fruit. Sporadically, I dated someone I had met there. I also recalled into service a hustler I used to see, and recruited a new one. None of them compared to Gabriel.

When my mini-affair with my bathhouse acquaintance came to an end, I called Gabriel. I told him that we could do deeds again, provided that there would be no drinking on his part at all in the house. He was delighted. His trip to Germany had to be postponed because his telephone-paying gentleman was out of the picture. At this crucial moment, when calls to Germany were a must, the penny-pinching phone company was going to pull the rug out from under him for the measly $567 he owed. This was also the time when he needed to prepare his wardrobe for his grand appearance in Wiesbaden to be presented to Wolfgang's friends.

I got rid of all the alcohol I had in the house. We fell into the same groove as before, with one difference. I did not see Gabriel exclusively. I would have preferred to spend all my sex money on him but did not want to put all my eggs into one basket.

Ever so slowly Gabriel's trip took shape. Obtaining a passport took many months. When he finally saved enough money for his ticket, it immediately disappeared into thin air and had to be reissued (this time sent to my address), delaying Gabriel's departure by many weeks. But, finally, in January of 1986 Gabriel was ready. We scheduled "The Last Deed." By the time I picked him up in the Castro district, he had already had a few drinks too many. Well, I thought to myself, let's celebrate in *his* style. Gabriel gave the session his all.

The next time I heard from him was in November of the same year. He made a noncollect call from his mother's home near Chicago.[3] Without a preamble explaining how he came to be with his mother in Illinois, he asked whether I would do him a favor. He wanted to know whether he could give my address and phone number as his residence once he returned to San Francisco. Gabriel and I had a psychic thing between us. We always read each other's thoughts. The suggestion that he would become my roommate panicked me. "Joseph," he said just as I was about to tell him that I would never live with him, "I am *not* going to stay with you. I just need to tell these people that I live with you."

"And who might 'these people' be?"

"The Probation Department."

"Why are you on probation?"

"I don't want to talk about it." There were many subjects that Gabriel did not want to talk about. For instance, whenever he lost a job he did not want to talk about the reasons for it. "I am afraid, Gabriel, you'll have to tell me about it, before I agree."

"I drove under the influence." This statement took me by surprise. Last I heard, Gabriel did not even know how to drive. "The probation forms will come to your home once a month. I'll come by to pick them up. You won't have to do anything at all."

I had known Gabriel long enough. Of course I would have to do lots of things. But he sounded so dejected and, yes, the moment I heard his voice I got a hard on. I agreed.

A week later he was at my place to tell me the entire story and, naturally, do a deed. Gabriel was broke, without a job and with no gentlemen holding safety nets underneath him. I raised the fee per deed to $35.

A few months earlier, Wolfgang and Gabriel had been tested for HIV and both came up positive. Wolfgang accused Gabriel of infecting him. He told Gabriel to go back to the States. Having no money and no place to go, and in a very depressed frame of mind, Gabriel flew to Illinois. The story of his DUI is too long to narrate, and would not make sense in any case.

Gabriel was fatalistic about his HIV status, though very upset about Wolfgang banishing him from Germany. He had done well for himself there, working illegally at a gay bar on a part-time basis. He also saw a number of wealthy *Herren* on the side.

In no time Gabriel resumed his previous lifestyle. He found a job, roommates to fight with, and a gentleman to look after his rent and utilities. He had no telephone, since he did not need to call Germany. (In order to have one installed, he would have had to pay his last phone bill, which he had neglected to do before leaving for Germany, plus a security deposit.) But there was one difference. As the gentleman grew frustrated with Gabriel's provocative behavior he abused him physically. The gentlemen who succeeded him did the same thing. Surprisingly, Gabriel took it in stride. *I* was more upset about his occasional black eye than he.

His probation "supervision" required Gabriel to perform only one task: once a month he had to send in a short form plus a certain amount of money to his probation officer. Almost monthly, something went awry involving me (as his putative roommate) in this procedure. There were many mistakes: Gabriel's papers did not arrive or were filled out incorrectly, he was tardy, the money order was for the wrong amount.

In this respect Gabriel behaved like many other street hustlers. The simplest tasks become major operations, with an endless stream of screw ups. Since Gabriel was gainfully employed there was no reason for him not to have a bank account. But Gabriel, like other hustlers, had had so many traumatic experiences with banks (more correctly, the banks had the traumatic experiences) that he chose not to open an account.

In the meantime, the impatient probation officer made threatening calls (to me) about revoking Gabriel's probation. Because his roommates would not take calls for him, and he could not be contacted at work, I would have to make heroic efforts to deliver his probation officer's threats.

I did many favors for Gabriel. Periodically, he had to find new accommodations and would ask me to help him move. When he wanted to escape his roommates and his gentleman, and just watch TV, we would do a deed, and then he would stay at my place as long as he wanted. I know that I was really his only friend. As soon as my phone became operable after the 1989 Loma Prieta earthquake, Gabriel was on the line. I found out later that I was the only person he had called.

What took me by surprise was Gabriel's reluctance to reciprocate by doing an odd favor for me. This has been my experience with quite a few other hustlers. My interpretation of this phenomenon is that both hustlers and clients are ambiguous about their roles. In theory—at least my theory—the hustler is an independent contractor, who charges handsomely for his services. In practice, it suits the hustler to convey the impression that he is a poor sex worker, who has to sell his body to survive. Why else would he receive a generous tip? (Independent contractors are not given tips for performing excellent work. Have you ever tipped your dentist?)

The client, too, may be happier with a hustler who is in a somewhat servile position. Helping a struggling young man financially, and obtaining sexual favors in return, may be less jarring to the client than buying it from a self-sufficient professional.

This ambiguity expresses itself in many ways. Half the time hustlers get their pay in an envelope, as if it were a tip for the concierge for a discreet and somewhat shady service. Other clients leave the money on the table or on the hustler's clothes. Rarely is the money just handed to them the way one would pay a plumber or an electrician.

For Christmas, many private contractors send me tokens of their appreciation for doing business with them—calendars, bookmarks, cards. Hustlers, like servants, are given gifts for the holidays without expecting reciprocation on their part.[4]

Which brings me back to Gabriel. I never asked him for free sex in return for favors I did for him. But I felt entitled to call upon him when I needed help, such as in rearranging furniture. He was dismayed when I asked him to do some work for me for free. One year he gave me, in writing, his Christmas wish list. I said, "Gabriel, I will be happy to exchange gifts with you this Christmas. Do you mind if I give you my list?" No gifts were exchanged!

I have noticed that most hustlers are reluctant to reverse the cash flow from them to their clients even when etiquette requires it. Model Alfonso, about whom I have written earlier, who took pride in his social sophistication, is a good example. I was dating someone at the time and had not seen him for a few months. One day he called me, asking me to write a résumé and cover letter for a summer job he wanted to apply for. When I finished the draft, he suggested that we meet for lunch to discuss it. I wondered how he would handle the bill. Obviously, I was not going to treat him. It would have been nice had he offered to pick up the tab, especially since he was very successful at his hustling business, and held a part-time job. But he suggested that we split it. I am sure that with a friend he would have picked up the tab. With a client he simply could not bring himself to do it.

The hustlers' endless need to receive money from clients is magnified because they often do not know whether, at a given moment, they are rich or poor. In spite of all the money Gabriel took in from his job, from me, an occasional other client, and his gentlemen, at times he was so broke that he went hungry. Yet the clothes he wore when he came over put my own wardrobe to shame. His watch and jewelry, which disappeared from time to time when he was drunk and had to be replaced, were worth a small fortune. In this respect, Gabriel was not unique.

It may well be that Gabriel's troubles with co-workers and roommates were a result of his extreme neediness in every area of his life. He was simply too busy with his own travails to notice that others had needs too, and that he might be called upon to help them. In spite of this, he was superbly attuned to the needs of his sex partners and, at least with me, never tried to cut corners in our sessions.

When all is said and done, maybe Gabriel, Alfonso, and other hustlers see all their clients as johns. If a client is a nice john, the hustlers will provide the best sex in their repertoire for him. That is their way of reciprocating.[5]

Gabriel showed no symptoms of his HIV infection. He never consulted a doctor and took no medicines. He entertained negative thoughts, drank heavily, did drugs, practiced unsafe sex at times, and starved his body. Gabriel, like a number of other hustlers I had known, also was a borderline anorexic. Sometimes, when he weighed himself on my bathroom scale, he would wonder out loud whether his weight loss signaled the beginning of his decline, as he put it. But, confounding the experts who recommend healthy living for HIV-positive people, he never so much as caught a cold.

Some three years after the Wolfgang affair came to an end, Gabriel found a new boyfriend named York. Like Gabriel, York was an alcoholic. He held a sales job at a department store and was even more prone than Gabriel to buy expensive and needless stuff. They constantly exchanged very expensive gifts, owed each other huge amounts of money, and impoverished each other. When they got drunk, a regular occurrence, York would sometimes batter Gabriel.

Surprisingly, York refused to live with Gabriel, which would have saved both of them some money. They had different work schedules. In order for them to see each other, Gabriel had to give up his gentleman because their schedules conflicted with the time he could spend with York. Pretty soon, without a safety net, Gabriel's financial situation collapsed altogether.

My schedule was much more flexible than Gabriel's gentleman's. He spent more time at my place than he had before meeting York because he really had no place to relax. York's roommates hated Gabriel and would not allow him to be there when York was at work.

York knew about me. Gabriel explained to York that he spent so much time with me because he was helping me with writing one of my travel guidebooks. When Gabriel showed York the published work he asked, logically, why I had made no mention of my hardworking assistant.

Gabriel's relationship with York was fraught with lies and withheld information.[6] The most important issue, their respective HIV status, was never discussed. When I asked Gabriel whether he practiced safe sex, he was annoyed by my question. "We try to do our best, Joseph. It is not always easy." (Gabriel and I had been practicing strict safe sex from our first meeting. He was as conscious of it as I. The first time he shaved at my place, after his HIV diagnosis, he discarded the blade. I would never have thought about it. Eventually, he bought a pack of disposable razors and kept them at my place.)

That things worked out between Gabriel and myself at all was due, in no small part, to the fact that he did not need, or even want, to impress me with anything more than his sexual performance. With me he could be himself. I knew, for example, how terribly broke he was in spite of his magnificent wardrobe! Before he went to Germany he asked me, somewhat sheepishly, to teach him how to knot a necktie. "I would be very embarrassed to ask anybody else to show me how to do this," he confessed. I knew, and did not care, that he was not as sophisticated and well-bred as he pretended.

Needless to say, I was not about to impress him as being very wealthy, as his sponsoring gentlemen did unfailingly. When my sex budget was exhausted, I would ask him for an "end of the month special." He always obliged, because he needed the money and, after doing the deed, he could stay at my place and watch TV.

All of this came to an abrupt end in 1991. One day York beat up Gabriel seriously enough for him to wind up at the emergency room of San Francisco General. After that incident, they split, and Gabriel went into a state of deep depression. He finally took advantage of his HIV-positive status and sought counseling. He may have seen the same therapist that Jed had consulted. As a first therapeutic step, she recommended to him that he stop being a "sex object."

For me it was a *déjà vu* experience. Unlike Jed, I knew Gabriel would change his mind because he would be unable to make ends meet without hustling. The therapist had deprived him of his means of livelihood without teaching him new skills (like money management). When he called me a few months later and suggested we resume doing deeds, he was utterly broke, had only a part-time job, and lacked a sponsoring gentleman. For a change, I was in my dating mode and was getting it for free much of the time.

By that time, I had no desire to resume my relationship with Gabriel. I had been very disturbed by the abuse he took from York.

I was also disappointed by his willingness to take the therapist's advise to stop being a "sex object" and, at the time, continue to be battered. (She counseled him to try to work things out with York.) As in Jed's case, I knew that once a shrink tells a hustler that making money this way is the source of his mental anguish, it will forever after be on his mind when he conducts his business.

I lost touch with Gabriel until I ran into him a few years later. He was in a halfway house learning how "not to use." He looked very thin and a lot older. I do not know whether his HIV had become symptomatic.

My six years with Gabriel were a case of having my cake and eating it. I had excellent sex with him at a price I could afford. Nobody ever got free sex from Gabriel—not even his boyfriend Wolfgang. At least I got it at an affordable price, in a forthright and honorable manner.

I could have saved a lot of money by not having Gabriel in my life. I could have gone to baths and sex clubs instead, and gotten it on, over and over again, with men I had no interest in. The money I spent on Gabriel was an excellent investment in my sexual well-being. For his part, Gabriel received not only my money but all sorts of help. Contrary to his therapist's views, it had been a good deal for both parties.

Chapter 11

A Monthly Arrangement

In my experience, dating hustlers has three advantages over meeting guys at the baths. First, the hustlers I pick are always my physical type. (I would not engage a hustler I do not care for physically. At the baths, by necessity, I compromise a lot.) Second, if I have sex with a hustler more than once, we are physically compatible. (At the baths availability takes precedence over compatibility.) Third, hustlers who are my type and with whom I am compatible are available to me when *I* want and need them.

There is a belief out there that it is a dreadful experience for men or women to have sex when they do not desire it, or with a partner not of their choosing, even if it is consensual. I have never understood why having to perform sexually as a job is, physically or psychologically, worse than, for instance, having to work in a coal mine eight hours a day.

But I know little about mining. Maybe coal miners go down the mine shaft with a song in their hearts. Let's take working at the baths, about which I know a lot more, as an example. Over the years, I have not only observed bath attendants at work, but also had sexual flings with a number of them. I know quite a bit about their working conditions. I am referring here to the workers who change the cum-stained sheets, dispose of the used condoms, and clean the shower stalls and the toilets. If I had to choose between having daily sex with Jack (the guinea pig in my hustler experiment), or working eight hours as an attendant in a bath house, I would opt for the former.

Even though having sex with Jack (or anybody else I did not care for) would be distasteful and tedious, it would have many advantages over an attendant's job. It would shorten my workday by seven hours. It would be physically less taxing and safer. (Attendants are exposed to everything from bodily fluids to used needles.) And, most important, I would not be subject to the pressures of patrons waiting for rooms, co-workers goofing off and expecting me to do their jobs, and the manager giving me a hard time.

I write all of this because part of the job description of a hustler is to perform sexually when the client desires it, the same way that a cabby picks up a fare when flagged or dispatched. As long as a hustler has control over his working hours and can elect *not* to get it on with certain clients, it is a job like any other job.

From the very beginning of my dealings with hustlers, I have been resentful about the size of their fees. This resentment has been based, primarily, on the percentage of my total income that I have been spending on hustlers. But it has also been envy. As a teacher, school principal, community college instructor, court interpreter, and hypnotherapist, I have never been paid per hour as much as an average model.

For many years, I toyed with the idea of working out a sex-for-money arrangement with a gay college student not of the hustler discipline. Such an arrangement would guarantee him a monthly income in return for a stipulated number of sexual sessions. I would pay him, say, four times his hourly wage in his part-time job, and guarantee him a fixed number of sessions per month. This way he would earn more and I would pay less. I thought this would be an especially good deal for a student who needed to augment his income with a minimum expenditure of time. Such an agreement could not be made with hustlers or models because they are used to taking in much larger amounts of money per session.

Two considerations deterred me. I did not want to commit myself to a fixed number of paid sessions because, albeit *very* rarely, I found free, satisfactory sex partners. And suppose, however unlikely, I found a permanent boyfriend. What would I do with the hustler I had retained on a monthly basis? I also realized that if I guaranteed a fixed number of sessions to a student, he would have to have sex with me on a regular schedule. He would, in effect, become my part-time employee. This would bring with it the usual squabbles between employees and their bosses.

The end of my relationship with Gabriel coincided with a reduction of my visits to the baths. I resigned myself to the fact that, at the baths, I would never find a boyfriend who would rescue me from hustlers. Neither of Gabriel's two understudies was good enough to take over his role on a permanent basis. I felt I needed a radical change. I started advertising for a "Mutually beneficial arrangement, ideal for a student."

My ad campaigns brought astonishing results, though no arrangement. Most surprising were the large number of replies and the economic status of some of the respondents. My ads were placed in two freebie nongay papers. This maneuver brought in quite a number of bisexuals who would not even have read the gay papers, in addition to many gay respondents. Since I did not ask for free samples, and I was not about to pay for sex seven days a week, some applicants had to wait a month for a trial session. (These sessions were scheduled after applicants had done well on a telephone interview, followed up by a personal meeting in a café.)

Quite a few respondents were not struggling young students. They were older professionals, earning decent salaries, such as a psychiatric social worker, a teacher, a court clerk. They loved the idea of selling their bodies![1] The money was only part of it. The adventure of prostituting themselves was a big turn on. It was, of course, a controlled adventure. Unlike real hustlers, they could always bring the experiment to a halt.

Among the younger respondents were quite a few first-year college students who wanted to have sex with an older man. The money was a lure as well as a justification.

The older professionals were well above the "thirty years old" limit I had specified in my ad. One of them, who claimed to be twenty-nine, was a schoolteacher. I did get it on with him a number of times. He was very much into pleasing and, though not exactly my physical type, was a very pleasant companion, with a great sense of humor. Our intellectual conversations made up for the lack of instant attraction. I met him in April. As soon as the school year came to an end, he decided to move East. He only wanted to earn extra income for a few months before his move.

With all the young college students I experienced the same problem. I'll write here about Sean, the one I liked best. Sean was only the third or fourth redhead in my life. He was a very clean-cut, outgoing, bisexual, WASPish preppie, twenty years old. He was into sports, especially tennis, and his physique showed it. Sexually he was interested in women his own age, and much older men. However crazy this may sound, he treated *me* as a sex object—any other man my age would have done just as well. Sean would never have permitted a man his own age to have sex with him, however much money the latter offered! There was a tremendous expenditure of sexual energy between us because Sean was so much into the sexual act with an older guy.

Like a street hustler, Sean would not keep appointments. He would try to fit me into a convenient time slot which, when the time came, he would try to change to another day. He had held all sorts of jobs before. I am absolutely certain that he took more liberties as a sex worker than in any other job. Even though he got paid much better by me than on his other jobs, he never understood that having sex was a job like any other.

I was surprised that I ran into this attitude with so many of the applicants. I am convinced that if I had interviewed them for a position such as a part-time driver, they would have understood that they would have to adhere to a schedule suiting my needs.

After interviewing many applicants, over a long period, I concluded that an arrangement would work only with someone who had served an apprenticeship as a model. I resigned myself to the fact that recruiting a former model would be a more expensive proposition because of his greater financial expectations.

In the meantime, when not interviewing, I saw my regular models who gave me a quantity discount. They were far superior to anybody I would have met at the baths, but not exciting enough for an "arrangement."

One day I was reading the model ads in the local gay paper when the following ad caught my attention:

> Haitian/East Indian, youthful, 5′10″, 137 lbs.,
> dancer's body, very affectionate, $80, out only.

Eureka! I exclaimed. I hit the jackpot. Everything I could possibly want in *one* package!

Many years earlier, I had visited Haiti. In those days it was ruled by the ruthless dictator François Duvalier (Papa Doc) with his secret Gestapo-like police, the Tonton Macoutes, brutally enforcing his regime. There was something about Haitian men, in conjunction with the tropical setting, that maddened me with raw lust. I had heard a lot about the Tonton Macoutes. Driven by my lust, I chose to disregard them completely, going merrily about my cruising.

Many East Indians live in Haiti, as well as in other Caribbean countries. I have no idea how much intermarriage there is between Haitians and East Indians. But I know that the offspring of such marriages are very appealing to me. I am fascinated by their looks, and even more so by their very dark skin, which resembles burnished copper. Any model who described himself as Haitian/East Indian would be on my short list.

And now, in front of me, was a model's ad, reminding me of so many joyful experiences. To top it all, the ad stated that he was "affectionate," the attribute I cherish most. It took three days, and many beeps, for the model to call back. Finally, my phone rang right after I beeped him. "I am Etienne. Did you beep me?" he asked.

I am very voice conscious. Etienne had a soft, sweet voice. He pronounced his name as a Francophone would. He said that he was a dance student, very slim and very dark. He was born in Haiti but raised in Miami. "I got dreads," he said, as if this would tip the scales one way or another. Actually, it did. More and more Etienne appeared to be a made-to-order model. I am crazy about dreadlocks.

"How old are you, Etienne?"

"I am twenty-five, but I look eighteen."

"I would very much like to see you," I said.

"I have a very busy schedule." There was long, inexplicable silence. "Can you pick me up at three o'clock tomorrow in front of my dance studio? It is on Franklin Street right off Market."

I agreed to pick him up, and gave him a description of my car. Before we ended the conversation he asked in a serious voice: "Do you know how to spell Etienne?"

"I think so." I spelled it for him.

"You forgot the accent on the first 'E.' It's Étienne."

"I'll remember this," I said.

Franklin Street is a major traffic artery. There was no parking available near Étienne's dance studio. Double parking was out of the question. I stopped the car some thirty yards north of the building by a fire hydrant, and waited, inside the vehicle, for Étienne. I kept looking in the rearview mirror watching for him. After ten minutes, I assumed he had stood me up. I was absolutely sure I had the right address because a large sign on the first floor read The Hip & Hop Dance Studio. I was pretty disappointed. I decided to give it another five minutes.

I had just started the car, when I saw in the mirror someone I assumed to be Étienne walking out of the building. As if guided by an inner radar, he turned left and walked up to my car. He let himself in and, in his sweet voice, asked, "Have you just arrived?"

My anger dissipated, giving way to a feeling of gratitude to the universe that it had created a man so much to my liking. I don't know how to describe Étienne objectively. Later, when I would ask friends who had met Étienne what they thought of him, they invariably said something like, "He's OK," or "You like them exotic-looking, don't you?" Just a while ago, my best friend saw me looking at Étienne's photo. "You must admit," he said, "that Étienne was really *medio feo.*" This quaint Spanish designation of "half ugly" adds some redeeming qualities to a person's basic homeliness. I concede that Étienne may not have been handsome by normative standards. For me, and his other admirers, he was the cutest guy in the world. For us he was an *homme fatal.*

Étienne did, indeed, look like an eighteen-year-old. Each of his dreadlocks had some blond hair woven into it, accentuating his far-out looks. The dreads also added to his androgynous appearance. In the car he was not very talkative. He never apologized for being late. I tried to keep up a conversation while I drove back home.

Étienne was born in Port-au-Prince—he pronounced the name of Haiti's capital the French way—but moved to Miami with his mother and his siblings at an early age. He had never met his East Indian father.

"Do you speak French?" I asked.

He thought my question over for a good half a minute. As I was to learn later, Étienne sometimes would mull over very simple questions for a very long time. "Yes," he finally said, "but I forgot much of it."

As soon as I asked, I realized it was a stupid question. Only upper-class Haitians speak French. The rest speak Creole. As a matter of fact, while we were seeing each other, Étienne never uttered a single French word.[2]

He finally perked up when I talked about hypnosis. He urgently needed to be regressed to his past lives. There, in one of his many past lives (he was a very old soul, he told me), he would find the key to his present existence.

When we came home, we sat in the living room for a while. I served Étienne juice. When he spoke, he moved his fingers, hands and forearms at very sharp angles, reminding me of East Indian dancing. I was fascinated by the elegance of his movements, even when just sitting down.

Étienne said that he needed to take a shower because he was very sweaty after his class. Only when he came out of the shower, stark naked, did I realize how sexy his body was. He had worn extra large clothes—the fashion among the young these days—making it impossible to get an accurate impression of what his body looked like under the oversized clothing. Now I was certain that, had I been allowed to choose a model from a thousand photos in a catalog, Étienne would have been my first choice. He had a cherubic expression on his face which, as I would soon find out, could easily change to impish and even mean. There was not an ounce of fat on his hairless, dark body, though his small and firm butt was prominent. His circumcised penis was small too. Because of the size of his dick, I doubt that his nude photo would have graced a thousand-model catalog!

I have disclosed so many of my heresies in this book that I might as well confess one more. I prefer partners who are not well hung. Needless to say, since this is my preference, I tend to meet hugely hung guys. Étienne was a very pleasant exception. I am sure that for him, comparing himself to other Haitian men, the small size of his dick must have occasioned some very traumatic experiences.

When we lay down I embraced Étienne. Belying his thinness, his body was enormously strong and supple. "Not so fast, buster," he said. "I run this show."

Having sex with Étienne was like taking a dance class. We started with warm-up exercises and progressed slowly to more complicated steps. Étienne kept correcting my style. "You don't know how to kiss."

"Teach me," I said. For the next year and a half, I took kissing lessons from Étienne. I was not a good student. I would slip into my old kissing habits, which Étienne considered dilettantish. But I'll say this for Étienne: each sex session he choreographed, ending with both of us climaxing simultaneously, was a very memorable experience. Étienne was nothing like Jed or Gabriel. Having sex with him was a learning experience: I perfected my style as a sex partner by doing it with a trainer.

While Étienne was teaching me sex techniques we also talked about his life. He told me that he had run his model ad only four times over a period of eight weeks, and had had about six clients. He was disappointed in all of them. Their sex techniques were shaky.

With me, it was different. Even though I was a slow learner, at least I tried to improve myself and, to the best of my limited ability, followed instructions. "I am bisexual," Étienne said. "I have had gay sex for only a year." I found this difficult to believe.

Étienne, who came to the United States when he was eight years old, had the slightest accent in English. It became much more pronounced when he was tired. It was not a French accent but, to me, it was just as charming.

"Will you regress me to a past life?" Étienne asked me after we climaxed.

I do not hypnotize for free. Just as I do not expect free sex from hustlers, I want them to pay me for my professional services. I told Étienne that he would have to pay for a past-life regression. "How much do you charge?" he asked.

"Fifty dollars per session."

One of Étienne's long silences ensued. It reminded me of a slow computer. The answer is there, but the computer takes a long time to spit it out. "Would you like to see me again?" he finally asked.

"Of course, Étienne. We need to work on improving my kissing techniques."

"How about you paying me $30 plus a hypnosis session next time?"

This is how Étienne and I started seeing each other regularly. The $30 became his established fee, and he was entitled to past-life regressions as needed. The lower fee was also based on a technicality. For Étienne, only a penetrative act qualified as sex. Étienne classified our sessions as massage. Within a month, he was the only hustler I saw. And I became his only client.

Étienne had not been very successful as a hustler. To begin with, his schedule was so hectic that most clients could not accommodate him. But the real problem was Étienne's schoolmarmish attitude. There was only one correct way to do things in bed—his way. I am not saying that he dictated *what* we did (that was left up to me) but *how* we did things was choreographed by him in minute detail. If, in the heat of passion, I took his hand and tried to wrap it around my penis, he would freeze, and then ask severely: "What are you doing?"

"I am taking your hand and moving it toward my penis."

"Are you trying to run this show?"

"No. I am just trying to enjoy myself." Étienne's face would assume a mean expression, he would give me a withering look, and return his hand to its previous resting spot. A few minutes later, when *he* was good and ready, he would wrap it where I had wanted it.

I suspect that most clients were turned off by his demeanor. I let him have his way. I liked Étienne so much that even letting him have complete control in bed turned me on.

I have already written about the dangers of finding a "dream hustler," someone who is exactly one's type. It makes the client ignore all of the hustler's shortcomings. I had been very attracted to Jed and Gabriel sexually, and I considered both of them cute. But they were not *precisely* my types and I was not completely powerless with them.

Étienne was my archetype! His face, body, movements, voice, penis, and even his androgyny were made to order for me. (Literally made to order. I prefer circumcised partners, and Étienne had been circumcised in his teens for medical reasons.) He was not a hustler who could be exchanged for another when the necessity arises, just as the Mona Lisa cannot be traded for another painting.

During the year and a half that we saw each other, I went abroad three times. Even though I got it on with local hustlers there, I missed Étienne terribly. Nobody measured up to him. Once, after arriving in Puerto Rico from Barbados, I called his answering machine just to hear his voice.

At the end of the second month of our acquaintance, Étienne asked whether he could borrow $100 to help pay his rent on the first of the month. By that time I was thinking again about a monthly arrangement. We did fewer past-life regressions (because he was rushed or tired and because I was bored and did not push the issue), and I was afraid he would raise his fee. The $30 per session fee I could afford, there was no hustler on the horizon I would like better, and no boyfriend lurking around waiting to supplant him. I decided to make him a formal offer.

I prefaced my offer by sharing with him my concern that our arrangement would change his status from independent contractor to employee. This fine distinction was lost on him. I said, "My proposal is that we would meet ten times a month—every third day. I will pay you $100 on the first of the month, and $20 every time I see you. If there are extra sessions, I'll pay the full $30."

Étienne mulled this over for a very long time. Then he said, "Because of my schedule I don't know if I can see you every third day. I am starting a new class. I'll be on a time frame."

Étienne used the expression "time frame" frequently. It meant that he was on a tight schedule. His meager income was derived from four sources: a dance class he taught in San Rafael that brought in $30 a week, minus his transportation expenses; working as a go-go dancer on the platform of a club; a part-time job selling clothes in a gay boutique; and the money that I paid him. Fortunately for him, he had a work-study job at his school doing clerical work there. My offer would almost cover the rent for his room.

I was surprised that he hesitated to accept my proposal. "Well, Étienne, I will try to accommodate your schedule. With goodwill, I think it's a can-do situation. After all, we have been seeing each other every third day for quite a while now. Why don't we try it for one month?" He agreed.

I believe that Étienne's schedule saved me from asking him to become my lover. I was so enraptured by him that I would have ignored our considerable age difference. But not even a much younger man could have kept up with him. Étienne had no fixed time for sleeping, eating, even for going to the bathroom. He was even more anorexic than Gabriel. Sometimes he would forget to eat for an entire day. On a Monday morning, for instance, he would come home from clubbing at 5 a.m., and sleep until eight. Then he would work at the boutique until 3 p.m. I would pick him up there and we would have a session. Around 6 p.m., he would take a nap at my place for an hour, then go to school, and then again to the clubs.

Often he would oversleep because he was exhausted and miss work, class, or an appointment with me. Or he would be late because he had to go the bathroom that very minute—he had neglected to take care of it for two days. If his boss or teacher or I scolded him for not being on time he would be very offended. He said that nobody understood or cared how little time he had to sleep. Squeezed into this schedule were his boyfriend and two or three other men. At least, as a client, I got a *lot* more sex than they did!

Étienne had not been a pharaoh or even a general in the ancient Egyptian army in the previous incarnations we explored. His past lives had a dreamlike quality. Étienne found them fascinating, and believed they had great significance. A Jungian analyst would have a field day with this material. I found it a bore. I am a Taurus (as Étienne, an Aries, constantly reminded me when he wanted to put me down) and therefore much too practical. I thought that Étienne should concentrate on the monumental obstacles he confronted in his present incarnation, rather than waste his time exploring the previous ones.

As I saw it, Étienne was in very deep trouble. Whichever move he made would result in a checkmate. Étienne Patel (he was given his father's surname), his mother, and his three younger siblings had been admitted to the United States provisionally as political refugees. Étienne's half brothers were of different fathers, and all bore their mother's maiden name. Somehow, when the family was processed for permanent residence, Étienne's name was dropped. The mistake went unnoticed. Subsequently the family split, and Étienne went to live with an aunt. When the time came for him to get his own ID, he did not have a shred of paper to prove his status.

Every now and then, Étienne made feeble attempts to get his papers in order. The last time, in Miami, he was apprehended by the INS right in their building as an illegal alien. He managed to slip away. They would probably have deported him, I assume to Haiti, though Étienne did not have any papers to prove where he was born.

As a result of this mess, Étienne could not obtain a legitimate Social Security card. He had bought a fake one in Miami, which bore his real name. As I understood it, the card's number was legitimate, but belonged to another person. With this, and an old photo ID issued by a Florida community college, he could secure jobs with small employers. Larger employers and government agencies were not fooled by his documentation. Since California matches names with Social Security numbers, Étienne could not obtain a driver's license in this state. His passion was driving. Every time he sat behind the steering wheel (he drove his school's van), he risked being cited for driving without a license and bad things would snowball from there.

Some of his fellow students had been recruited by a Dutch nightclub on a year's contract. Étienne could have gone with them, but he was unable to obtain an American passport. He probably could not even have obtained a Haitian passport—he was a man without a nationality.

I saw Étienne in a few presentations with his school. He performed highly choreographed versions of hip hop and street dancing. I considered him a very gifted dancer. But, as a dancer, he had no future even as a common hoofer. He had auditioned many times and was rejected, apparently, because he had the wrong body type. (I was never quite clear about this point.) Had he been accepted, his phony Social Security card would have trapped him sooner or later.

With my practical Taurus mind I wanted to help him deal with his major problem. At one time, I told him that I would pay immediately for a consultation with an immigration lawyer, and suggested withholding $5 every session to cover the legal fees. He was all for it in principle, but I could not persuade him to get in touch with his aunt so she could contact his mother to find out whether there were any Étienne Patel documents in existence. Nor was he willing to give up $5 per session to pay a lawyer. Taking care of his legal status was of much less concern to Étienne than exploring a previous life or even checking out a new club.

I was both right and wrong that Étienne would resent becoming my employee. The sex did not bother him at all. Once, after a fight with his boyfriend, he idly speculated whether he should be monogamous with me. Our lovemaking was just as satisfying to him as it was to me. It was his inability to deny me sex on a whim that disturbed him. With his on-and-off boyfriend and sundry other admirers he would routinely refuse sex even when he shared the same bed with them.

I was again in the strange position where I knew much more about Étienne than his boyfriend. I had run into the latter many times, while picking Étienne up from his home, and was presented as The Hypnotist. He was a good-looking young guy who eventually had a nervous breakdown. I suspect Étienne "helped" him into this state. Although the boyfriend knew next to nothing about the real relationship between Étienne and myself, I knew all about the boyfriend, as well as about Étienne's other mini-affairs.

We did have sex more than ten times a month. Some months have thirty-one days and required an additional session. At other times, we had "emergency" sessions when I felt that I needed to see him more often than every third day. Curiously, Étienne preferred the extra sessions—they were optional under the terms of our contract. He never refused them, because he needed the money and, I believe, he enjoyed them as much as I did.

Étienne understood perfectly that the encounter every third day could not be postponed to accommodate his schedule. He did not object to the frequency. But we would adjust the hours to work within his erratic schedule. We would plan on having sex at 9 a.m. on a Tuesday and at 7 p.m. on a Friday. In practice, the morning session started at noon because he overslept, and the evening meeting would be postponed by two hours because he missed the bus from San Rafael.

As I had predicted, Étienne harbored the grudges employees have against their employers. If he could but tell me on one of the obligatory third days, while in my home, "Today we won't have sex. Maybe in three days from now, we will do it," he would not have been so angry with me over trivialities.

This resentment expressed itself in many ways. He was always very affectionate and cuddly when we had sex. But if I tried to give him a good-bye hug in the garage before I drove him to school he would push me away. It was his way of stating that he did not want to work overtime.

No client is a hero to his permanent hustler. Frustrated with our arrangement, Étienne would pick on me, criticizing the way I drew the curtains or folded my clothes. This would often lead to bickering, ending in a verbal fight, with Étienne muttering what I took to be a Creole voodoo imprecation. Then, angrily, we would proceed to have sex. Like clockwork, the more we bickered and fought before our sexual session, the better and more tender it became.

Étienne told me once that his mother had sex with her many lovers while screaming at them and, sometimes, beating them up. Maybe Étienne was repeating this pattern. Such sessions did not resemble an encounter between a hustler and his john. They were like lovers making up.

The relationship between us was extremely complicated. I was more than infatuated with Étienne. I may even have loved him. I felt an obligation to rescue him from falling off the precipice on the edge of which he blithely danced. Sometimes I thought that Étienne, in his own way, loved me too, but I was crowding him, and he could not control me fully.

We did have a lot of good times. One evening when I picked him up, he was all smiles and goodwill. For the first and only time he fondled me in the car. When we were in bed he said, "Please take my buns today." I obliged, wondering what brought this about. That evening, I had the ideal Étienne. The next time around, he told me that he had taken an Ecstasy pill the previous time. He did this twice more. I am convinced that he would not have taken Ecstasy before having sex with me unless he had some sincere feeling toward me.

More than anything else, I appreciated his support of my caregiving for my former housemate, Jacinto. During my time with Étienne, Jacinto was slowly, very slowly, dying of AIDS. He was frequently in and out of the hospital. Some days I would visit him there twice. When Étienne had the time, he would go with me and try to cheer up Jacinto. These two liked each other. Étienne, though HIV negative, identified with Jacinto, who had similar legal problems. When Jacinto passed away, Étienne was very comforting, suspending his bickering for a few weeks.

I found many occasions to give Étiennne little presents. Not in a sugar daddy manner, but like a lover or a boyfriend. For instance, when he went on a vitamin-supplement kick (which lasted all of a month), I gave him a gift certificate to a health food store. Unlike other hustlers, sometimes he even gave me gifts. Étienne was not an educated person, and, except for kissing and sex techniques, he had little to teach me. Yet I wanted to be with him sexually and even socially as often as possible.

I do not know how bisexual Étienne really was. But he had many women friends of all ethnic groups. He often rented a room in one of their homes. He kept moving from one place to another. Usually, he lived in good neighborhoods. Then he moved to Eddy Street in the Tenderloin district, a pretty bad neighborhood. Eddy Street was a dangerous place to wait for Étienne while parked in a fire hydrant zone reading a newspaper. We had so many fights over his tardiness that at the end of the month we decided not to renew our contract.

Our separation lasted all of three weeks. I took up with Gabriel's understudies, who were happy to see me again. I felt disappointed with each session. In the meantime, Étienne's roommate threatened him with eviction for not paying his rent. Étienne and I renewed our arrangement. I raised him to $350 per month, with the understanding that, henceforth, he would be more punctual.

Eventually, stressed out completely by his tardiness, I raised him to $400. In return, he would arrive at my home by public transportation; at the end of the session, I would drive him home or to school. Half the time, Étienne took taxis to my place, canceling out both raises. Even with taxis he was late. But at least I was waiting for him in the comfort of my home.

Then, within a period of ten days, three calamities descended upon Étienne. His *raison d'être* in this city was his dance school. One day he was told that his work-study job would not be renewed. A few days later, his employer at the boutique received a letter from the Social Security Administration asking him to correct Étienne Patel's number. His boss had known about Étienne's problem, but, upon receiving the letter, got cold feet and told Étienne that he could not work at the boutique after the end of the month.

The third blow was the worst. Étienne, like so many other young men and women I know, went to Rave parties once or twice a month. Étienne was a moderate consumer of recreational drugs, but would go all out at these Raves.

After being told that he would be laid off, he started interviewing for another position. He carried his ID and phony Social Security card with him to the Rave. There he did heavy-duty drugs. He must have fallen asleep at some point. When he woke up his beeper and wallet were gone.

Étienne was so devastated by these experiences that he decided to return to Miami. There his aunt ran a rooming house of sorts, and Étienne could always stay with her and help with the chores.

I had to will myself *not* to invite Étienne to become my roommate. That would have taken care of his rent. The $400 I paid him monthly would cover his tuition and leave him with some spending money. And, like so many other undocumented aliens, Étienne could, perhaps, find a job where papers were not required.

"You are not Étienne's lover for better or for worse," I kept repeating to myself. "He has always been your hustler and you have fulfilled all your obligations toward him." Having Étienne as a roommate *and* hustler would have been much more than I could have handled. Like his lover, I would have had a mental breakdown.

At the end of July I drove Étienne to the bus station. I never heard from him again. I still miss him!

* * *

I learned a number of lessons from my arrangement with Étienne. First, that, given the right hustler, I would prefer having sex for money only with him. Second, that while I can have a de facto arrangement, it must not be contractual. (I know this sounds confusing, but I will explain this fully in the last chapter, when describing my present arrangement.) Third, that I should never again play chauffeur to hustlers.

The most important lesson I had known long before meeting Étienne. Clients should not fall in love with their hustlers, but it happens!

In retrospect, I view the Étienne Patel affair as a successful, though sad, hustler liaison. There was much more than sex between Étienne and myself. There was passion!

Chapter 12

Health and Safety

Casual sex at clubs or baths, or picking up men at random in parks and bars, exposes you to more health risks than having safe sex with hustlers.

Gay author Michelangelo Signorile has repeated the same story in numerous TV and radio interviews.[1] On a trip to Hawaii, he met a hunk. When the time came, he did not insist on safe sex because he was afraid that the hunk would walk out on him. He rationalized his behavior in many ways—the hunk was in the military and therefore must be HIV negative.

A hustler will not walk out on you because you insist on safe sex! Moreover, if the hustler himself is HIV negative, and not drunk or on drugs, he will insist that you practice safe sex. If he is positive and does not care, or if he is negative but you offer him more money, you may succeed in having unprotected sex. However, it will be your doing.

I have complained many times already that male hustlers are tarred with the same brush as female prostitutes. Historically, female prostitutes contributed to the spread of venereal diseases, and also do so presently with AIDS.[2] In the gay community, AIDS has spread primarily through free, promiscuous sex. In the line of duty, hustlers certainly are not exposed in one day to as many different men as a patron in a gay sex club.

I have been told by many hustlers that some clients, seeking unprotected sex, give them drugs or get them drunk. I have yet to hear from a client that a hustler insisted that they have unsafe sex.

Because of their economic situation most hustlers get inferior medical care compared to their clients, but in the case of venereal diseases, the opposite is true. In most metropolitan areas in the United Sates, and in many other countries, hustlers who need treatment can go to public

VD clinics. The doctors there are much more knowledgeable about these diseases than many of their colleagues in private practice. They are also smarter about patients' compliance—taking their medications as precribed.

To sum up: You do not need to worry about additional health risks when seeing hustlers (compared to nonpaid, promiscuous partners) *as long as you have protected sex.*

* * *

Things are not so simple when it comes to personal safety. Having sex with hustlers is not necessarily dangerous, but having sex with strangers can be. Men who are out to harm you are going to assure you that they are *not* hustlers. For example, in some Central American countries a guy you pick up in a bar will slip a mickey in your drink. Then, often after having sex with you, when you are fast asleep, he'll clean you out. When you met him, he assured you that he was not a hustler, so you would not reject him out of hand for this reason. As a matter of fact, all my bad experiences were with people who assured me that they were not hustlers. I'll write more about this subject later.

It is the act of cruising, and bringing strangers home, that is dangerous. However, it is also part of the excitement of gay life. The purpose of this chapter is to try to minimize the risks inherent in the game of meeting hustlers and models.

You may find that certain precautions I mention are not practical for you. For example, if your thing is to spend the night with a sex partner, my advice not to let strangers sleep with you is useless. Within what is comfortable for you, try to follow my safety tips.

LISTEN TO YOUR INTUITION

Your intuition is faster than your intellect in recognizing danger. Unfortunately, your intuition communicates obscurely. If you meet a stranger and plan on taking him home, it may tell you something like, "No, he is not OK because he seems out of place." If the guy in question happens to be the hottest man you have ever met, your intellect demands more of an explanation. However, this peremptory communication can save your ass, even your life.

It works the other way, too. Sometimes you meet a hustler who appears sullen and morose. Even though you like him, you feel endangered by his attitude. Your intuition may tell you that he is OK, in spite of his seeming unfriendliness. This has happened to me many times with hustlers who, eventually, turned out to be shy rather than morose.[3]

Always trust your intuition more than your logical analysis. Do not use logic to overrule your gut feeling. Do *not* experiment to see whether your intuition was correct!

INTERVIEW YOUR HUSTLER

To give intuition a chance to work you need time to interview the hustler. Many pickups are made by car. The client cruises in his car, stops in front of the hustler, and invites him into the vehicle.[4] It is much better to conduct these interviews on neutral ground such as the street. (If you are driving while interviewing the hustler, you have poor eye contact with him!) Even in cities such as Los Angeles, try to park the car and interview the hustler on the street.

I have observed the same phenomenon over and over again during the interview. Client and hustler exchange names. Then they engage in small talk, for example, "Where are you from?" or "It's a cold night." A few minutes into the small talk either client or hustler will ask, "What was your name again?" The interview initially consists of checking out the "vibes." What each party says is not as important as the general impression he makes. This time is essential to let intuition do its thing! Only after you feel comfortable with the hustler should you discuss the details of the sex act itself.

Do not make the mistake of assuming that a hustler would not be dangerous to you because he is no match for you physically. When bad stuff happens, it is not because you slug it out with the hustler and he wins. If you do not trust a hustler, do not overrule this feeling by saying to yourself that you will be able to take care of him if push comes to shove. The bad stuff is likely to be the pinching of some valuable item rather than pushing or shoving.

PREPARE YOURSELF

Some years ago, I stayed at a gay hotel in Acapulco. The only door to the compound was always locked from the inside after 6 p.m. To leave the hotel at night, a hotel employee would have to unlock the door. This arrangement would freak out an American fire marshal, but it was a simple and effective safety measure for guests. They could bring whomever they fancied to the hotel. If a guest's pickups wanted to leave the hotel, he needed the OK of the guest himself. The hotel owners wanted to prevent the major danger of bringing in strangers: theft.

Hustlers who steal from clients are, almost always, either opportunistic or vengeful. To a large extent, you can take steps to prevent such occurrences. Remember that as you get to know the hustler better, your intuition will tell you when and how much you can trust him. Once trust has been established, you can treat a hustler or a model the same way you treat other friends and acquaintances.

Here are some tips: When picking up a hustler, or meeting a model, don't have in your possession more money, credit cards, and documents than absolutely necessary. Leave your Rolex watch and jewelry in a secure place at home. Dress as modestly as possible. If you plan on having sex at the hustler's place, put his fee in a different pocket than the rest of your money. Don't bring along a hundred-dollar bill expecting the hustler to make change.

If you plan on bringing a hustler home make sure there are no money, jewelry, documents, or prescription (or recreational) drugs lying around. If you are, say, a senior vice president of a bank, secure your calling cards unless, of course, you want the hustler to call.

Remember that there will come a time during the session when you will be naked and will have to leave your clothes unattended, such as when going to the bathroom. Inside your pockets are your documents and cash. Work out a routine that will allow you to be away safely from your clothes for a few moments. If you need to take a shower after the session, drive the hustler home first, and do so later.

It is much better not to have a stranger stay with you overnight. Do *not* rely on the fact that you are a light sleeper, or that he will sleep entwined in your arms. If you must have him spend the night with you, hide your wallet and car keys.

Drink moderately and, if at all possible, do not do drugs. You are not in full control of the situation when on drugs. Also, you have no idea how the hustler will react to a given drug. Do you want to deal with his paranoia?

There are many clues about your financial status a hustler gets from just being at your home. It is not necessary to tell him that you are a very wealthy man, even if this happens to be true.

You are more vulnerable when you travel. A lot of gay travelers behave less cautiously when they are in a foreign country. Nobody knows them there. The trouble is that they also don't know anybody there who would be able to help them in case of an emergency. Often, they do not speak the local language.

Gay travelers who want to bring visitors to their hotel—in many countries this will be the only possible way to have sex—should leave all their valuables in the hotel safe or, better yet, bring as few of these items as possible on the trip. The only items of great value in the room should be the ones essential to the trip itself, such as a camera. These should be secured in a locked suitcase with the key hidden.

Spending money should also be well hidden, but not locked away. You may want to take the hustler out for a bite to eat after the session, and may need cash. Traveler's checks belong in the hotel's safety deposit box. Even more important, the passport and travel ticket should be there too.[5] Lately, I have been using a credit card with my photo as an ID when traveling abroad. If it is lost or stolen, I can cancel it with a collect phone call.

Because I like to carry more money on me while I am in a foreign country than at home, I wear an old-fashioned money belt. (This is a belt that has a zipped compartment, facing inward, to put bills in.)

COMMUNICATE FULLY

I have already written at great length about communicating fully and openly with the hustler or model about your expectations. It is also important that he feel that a fair deal has been struck. If a hustler quotes a ridiculously low fee I would be very suspicious of him. He may, however, be desperate to earn *some* money because he is hungry or needs to pay his overdue rent. If I feel comfortable with him, I will raise his fee beforehand so he will feel less inclined to "adjust" it sometime during the session. Inasmuch as possible, try to avoid causing a hustler to have a grudge against you.

* * *

In many countries the world over there are laws on the books against female prostitution. They are now routinely applied against males as well.[6] Attempts to enforce these laws are usually aimed at street hustlers rather than models. Like their female counterparts, male street hustlers affect the neighborhood negatively. No police force has ever been successful in eradicating prostitution. By harassing prostitutes of either gender, as well as their patrons, the police hope to contain the practice.

As I have written throughout this book, many street hustlers could not make a living by doing any other work, not only because they lack the skills, but because of their temperament. In a way, by working as hustlers they are doing society a favor. They are money-hungry young males who would embark on a career of *real* crime if they were unable to prostitute themselves. In some countries attempts have been made to license streetwalkers, for example Costa Rica, where both female and male street prostitutes (hustling in drag) must carry a *carnet*.[7] Unlike females who work for a pimp on a steady basis, males may be on the streets in one city today, and in another city tomorrow, or hustle once in a blue moon. Enforcing registration laws for male street hustlers would probably not work very well.

Because antiprostitution campaigns tend to be dormant for a long while and then become extremely aggressive—often driven by an upcoming election—cruising the streets for hustlers can involve a client with the forces of law and order. Afternoons, especially on Sundays and holidays, are less hectic, with fewer cops on the beat, but of course, with a smaller selection of hustlers.

Models are a much safer bet, though they are confined to large metropolitan areas where they can advertise their services. These days models can use voice mail, which is easier to obtain than telephone service. A lot of street hustlers, even without a permanent residence, have upgraded themselves to models. In localities where models can advertise, street hustlers nowadays are at the very bottom of the barrel.

When practiced by models on an individual basis (not through an agency), the laws against prostitution are rarely, if ever, enforced. There are so many ads, in such diverse publications—including, of late, the Internet—that enforcement, or even containment, would be impractical.

Given a city where one can summon advertising models compared to picking them up on the street, the former would be the safer way to go.[8] Still, precautions should be in place until the client gets to know the model better, over a period of time.

In general, it is safer to go to a hustler's or model's home than to have him come to your place. The S/M crowd figured this out a long time ago. Ordinarily, fewer calamities happen in the hustler's home. But having sex at the hustler's or model's home brings up a number of issues. First, how safe is his neighborhood and his residence? (Many hustlers live in slum hotels.) Second, if you have a car, will you be able to park there? (If there are parking meters, you will be limited in the time you can spend with the hustler, masseur, or model.) Third, does the hustler live in a place that is clean and conducive to a sex session?

Many clients are not in a position to weigh the relative advantages of an in versus an out call. Going to hustlers' homes is the *only* venue for clients who cannot entertain them in theirs, such as young guys who live with their parents, and married men.

It is extremely dangerous to bring two strangers home. If you want a threesome organize it yourself, with two hustlers you have known for a while or, at least, know one of them well. There are ads that feature two models working together. I would prefer to go to their place rather than have them at my home the first time around.

* * *

This chapter is being written after the murder of designer Gianni Versace by Cunanan. While he was a fugitive in hiding, his friends and acquaintances, going back to his high school days, were interviewed. It seemed that everybody had known all along that Cunanan was a pathological liar, not to be trusted.[9] Why then was he so popular with so many people?

This is where the "cuteness" factor comes in. We sometimes ignore warning signs if the perpetrator is, in our eyes, cute. This rarely happens with hustlers (at least, initially) because we are more careful with them. Cunanan's admirers met him socially, not in a street alley, and let down their guard.

I myself have run into a few guys whom I judged to be hustlers but who insisted that they were not. They were right—they turned out to be thieves and forgers, not sex workers. Not only my intuition but my observations and those of my friends classified these guys as bad news. Still, because I was getting it for free (I never paid them; I lent them money or gave it to them as a gift), I did not break with them at the first sign of dishonesty or chicanery.

These quasi-hustler relationships tend to bring about bad surprises. Invariably, the nonhustlers prepared their crimes well in advance. (Like stealing blank checks long before trying to pass them.) I am sure that in their own minds their acts had a justification: they had given me a lot of great sex for free and they just claimed their reward.[10]

Avoid hustlers masquerading as free sex partners. Their money "borrowing" will give them away.

Looking back at the many hundreds of hustlers and models I have been intimate with, some of whom were drug addicts, alcoholics, and mentally disturbed people, how is it that I had so few bad incidents with them?

I have always treated hustlers the way I treat anyone else. I don't put them on a pedestal, talk down to them, or interact differently with them than with other people. I do not aspire to be their boss, and I certainly do not lavish huge amounts of money on them. I do not try to get them to do more than we have agreed upon by getting them drunk or stoned. I talk with them a lot about their lives and about subjects that interest them.

Most important, I take it for granted that the session will work out the way it is supposed to. That is, I expect a competent sex worker to take care of my sexual needs in return for fair remuneration. An anecdote will illustrate this statement.

Some fifteen years ago, on a Sunday afternoon, I ran into Joe on Polk Street. Traditionally, hustlers stand on the east side of the street. He sat on the stairs of the building on the west side. He had the darkest eyes I had ever seen. Joe told me that he was half Native American and half Filipino. He attributed his dark eyes to having looked directly at the sun during an eclipse. "When I am fifty, I'll be blind."

"How old are you now, Joe?"

"Nineteen, man."

"Well, you have thirty-one good years left," I said.

Joe looked very exotic and, by my standards, quite cute. He was from Hayward and had come to San Francisco to make some money on the weekend. He was a short, affable, butch number. We agreed on Joe's fee and what we were going do sexually. While I drove home with him, making small talk, I suddenly had an intuitive flash: Joe was straight. I mean, Joe was straight in his own eyes.

"Are you straight or gay, Joe?" I asked conversationally.

"I'm straight, man."

This worried me. In those days I did not know about young men who, sexually, like young women and older men. I had not contracted with Joe to do what macho men do to queers: fuck them. What Joe and I had agreed to do in bed, from kissing to sucking, was what fags did to each other.

Joe said, "I want to ask your opinion about something."

"Go right ahead."

"I got my girlfriend pregnant. She is real pissed at me. She told me she would never let me see the baby. I want to punch her real hard in the stomach, make her lose the baby. What do you think, man?"

I reflected on this for a while. "Do you know about karma, Joe?"

"Yes, man."

"Well, what you want to do to your girlfriend and your baby is very bad karma."

We talked some more about his girlfriend. I think I managed to talk him out of aborting his baby. I thought someone else should take up with him the payment of child support.

When we came home I made him a cup of coffee. We talked for a while. Then I said, "Shall we go into the bedroom?"

Joe was a decent sex partner. He did exactly what we had agreed upon. Toward the end, he asked, "Do you want me to shoot my load, man?"

"If you want to, man." (We had not agreed on that beforehand.)

Joe shot. We dressed, I gave him his money, and took him back to Polk Street.

I suspect that if I had shown Joe that I was worried, or if I had played a hetero porno video to turn him on and then did my homo stuff, or if I had tried to convince him that he was bi, not straight, it could have become an ugly scene. I treated Joe as if I had contracted with him to paint a room. It was no big deal. He was not a low-life hustler, I was not a big-shot Polk Street john, we were not engaged in a mind-blowing ritual, and he did not need elaborate mental preparations to perform his job.

I have read many interviews with mountain climbers. They all say something like this: If a mountaineer knows what he is doing, makes sure to take the necessary precautions, and has reliable equipment, the sport itself is not particularly perilous. But it can become extremely dangerous when precautions are not in place.

Picking up hustlers involves some risks, many of which can be controlled by taking proper precautions. These precautions need to be taken the same way you fasten your seat belt when you start driving. You do not dwell on the dangers of driving and you do not anticipate an accident. You just follow standard operating procedures.

Chapter 13

Hustlers and Financial Well-Being

In the 1980s, I conducted self-hypnosis seminars at the College of Marin, less than an hour's drive from San Francisco. One of those seminars was called "Financial Well-Being Through Self-Hypnosis." In this seminar, I taught students the skill of self-hypnosis, so that they could apply it to finding meaningful jobs, purchasing the things they really needed and wanted, and earning an adequate amount of money to live comfortably in the style they chose.

A publisher's scout must have taken notice of my seminar. I received a letter from Prentice-Hall asking me whether I would write a book with the same title as the seminar.

I agreed. By and large, I wrote exactly what I had been saying in my classroom. A year later, my book was published.[1] The artful cover of the book had sixteen gold-colored dollar signs on it! I was interviewed on a number of radio talk shows. The hosts, having seen the book and its cover but not having read it, always started the interview by asking: "So, will hypnosis help our listeners become rich?"

I felt embarrassed. I was such a poor role model for teaching others how to become rich! Financial well-being is not the same as being rich. Many wealthy people live in a state of constant financial panic. They realize that the paltry millions they have amassed really amount to very little in these troubled times, and that even this amount can be wiped out when the stock market throws one of its tantrums.

What I do know a lot about is how to use money to obtain good and steady gay sex. Sex that, in my experience, would not be available to many gay men without the money. I will end this book by describing how, with relatively little money, I have been able to enjoy a very fulfilling, steady, and predictable sexual life with Étienne's substitute.

* * *

For a long while, Étienne was irreplaceable. Again I saw Gabriel's understudies—two average models with pleasant personalities. And, once again, I ran a furious ad campaign for free sex partners. This particular campaign brought into my life a crop of young guys who could barely find enough time to get away from their girlfriends to fulfill their kinky fantasies with an older man. This was free but highly unsatisfactory sex. It was rushed, secretive, and impersonal.

How could free sex with these young guys be more impersonal than with hustlers? Hustlers are hired to please the client. The ones who stay in business manage to do so. The kinky young guys are primarily interested in pleasing themselves. If they manage to please their partners in the process, it is a mere by-product. Jimmy, a bright nineteen-year-old student, is a good example. He wanted an older man—any older man—to stick a huge dildo up his ass. The foreplay I insisted upon was agreeable (maybe even pleasurable) to him, but was completely impersonal. It was rushed, because he wanted enough time for the dildo ritual. Once fulfilled, he would hurry back, unshowered, to his girlfriend and his studies. He never made a date for a future meeting. This would happen when, under pressure of exams, he needed the dildo in place. My needs were of no concern to him.

I came to the conclusion that I had to interview a crop of new models. The fourth one, Michael, became my permanent model. He is Dominican on his mother's side, and Puerto Rican on his father's. He is a quiet, somewhat shy, short, and slim young man. I think he is *very* cute and lovable, but probably not very comely by ordinary standards.

Michael ran away from his home in New York City and has been on his own since the age of thirteen. He has seen and done it all, and now, at the age of twenty-two, is a conservative guy, concerned with running his own life efficiently in order to live peacefully. He has given up on drugs and wild parties. He has a full-time job and hustles on the side.

Unlike most of my previous models, he is not an imperious queen and is very easy to get along with. He is concerned with controlling his own life, rather than, like Étienne and Gabriel, running other men's lives. Fiercely independent, he never asks for favors or money loans.

At our first meeting, we spent close to two hours just talking. Once he felt comfortable, Michael was a talkative guy with an incredibly colorful past. He has had an extremely hard and sad life, but has learned to take control of his affairs.

In bed, Michael's specialty is affection. We are sexually quite compatible. I was sure of this compatibility the first time around. At the end of our first session, I said to him, "Michael, I would really like to see you on a regular basis. We are looking at ten times a month. I cannot pay you $80 every time I see you."

"Well, what would you be willing to pay?"

"I give all my regulars $50 per session."

"That's OK."

Within a month I was seeing, on a paid basis, only Michael. By the end of the second month, I all but stopped my ad campaign.[2] He also reduced his own advertising drastically. These days he only sees, occasionally, his former regulars. Besides the good sex, what I appreciate most in Michael is his punctuality and his consideration. He takes public transportation to my place, and I drive him to the Castro district at the end of the session. If he is going to be late, he'll call me and let me know well ahead of time.

Michael has had less formal education than all my other long-term hustlers, yet he is the most responsible one. Unlike other models, who have the most modern communication capabilities (a cellular phone communicating with beeper and answering machine), all Michael has is an unsophisticated beeper. With only this gadget, he always manages to respond almost instantly to calls, and never, ever, screws up an appointment! The better-educated models, with their state-of-the-art communication capabilities, somehow manage to miss appointments quite frequently.

I have not repeated with Michael the mistake I made with Étienne. Even though I see him every third day, sometimes more often, we have no formal contract with each other. Both he and I can decline to see each other without explanations. So far, this has never happened.

It took a long time for Michael to open up fully. One day, I showed him some photos of me as a child. The next week, he brought photos of his friends, to whom he is close since they serve as his surrogate family. I found this a touching gesture on his part. He had spoken of them often but, of course, I would never get to meet any of them. As far as they know, Michael cleans my home every third day.

Recently, Michael and I celebrated our one hundredth session. (Yes, I keep track of such things!) Michael told me that I had been the steadiest client in his career. Most of his other regulars see him occasionally rather than exclusively. "They usually want someone new if they pay for it," he told me.

If at all possible, I have always preferred seeing only two or three hustlers on a regular basis. Lately, I have discovered that if I am completely compatible with a hustler I prefer seeing him exclusively. I derive comfort from our predictably harmonious interaction. Maybe this is a limited-liability boyfriend relationship. We are both on our best behavior when we are together, without having to put up with the inevitable upheavals and turmoil of permanent live-in boyfriends.

I have stated throughout this book that clients ought not mistake their hustlers for lovers. But when a client sees a hustler almost exclusively, and the hustler has only a few other clients, both parties must also like each other in a nonphysical way to make such an arrangement viable. Not all hustlers are good candidates for this sort of arrangement. Models with luxury apartments, costly accessories (such as S/M equipment), and fancy ads with photos do not want or need a limited-liability boyfriend relationship.

* * *

I planned on taking a two-week vacation at a small Mexican resort in August 1997. Before I left, I made a date with Michael for the day after my return from Mexico. I had no way of knowing how my sex life would play out there. For me, the greatest luxury was that I could assure myself of good sex immediately upon my return. Yes, it may have been better and more meaningful if I had a lover I could take along on my trip, or if upon my return my lover would wait for me at the gate to welcome me. Without a lover, seeing Michael was the next best thing.

Many gay men travel abroad for sexual odysseys. I have made such trips to Mexico, Japan, and the Philippines. The grass appeared greener there. (At one time or another I toyed with the idea of moving to these countries. I have studied Spanish, Japanese, and Tagalog.) I have friends who make annual sex pilgrimages to Asia, Central America, and Europe. Their entire sex life and discretionary budget are focused on these brief trips.

I have come to believe that by hook or by crook the center of one's sexual activities ought to be where one lives permanently. An adventure-filled fourteen-day vacation does not make up for fifty sexless and bleak weeks. In gay publications there are always ads from models of different nationalities and of all ethnic groups. Through models, one can bring a sexual utopia into one's own backyard.

* * *

My destination in Mexico proved to be a fishing "village" called Playa del Carmen, on the Yucatán peninsula, an hour's drive south of Cancún. By now it is really a town with many hotels. All I wanted was to be in a warm place—summers in San Francisco are cool and foggy—and swim in the ocean.

I spent three nights in Cancún. The second night I went to a gay bar. All over the world, and especially in Mexico, gay bars are more suitable for vampires than for people who need to go to work (or the beach) the next day. When I arrived at the bar, at 10 p.m., it was not even open. Among the few patrons waiting for the bar to open was Javier. We were not each other's type, but while we waited we passed the time chatting. He steered me to a gay hotel in Playa del Carmen.

At 10:30 the bar finally opened. I ordered drinks for Javier and myself, and then made feeble attempts to cruise the few suitable partners. (At that "early" hour the bar was far from full.) The music was so loud that I had to shout in order to converse. By midnight, I tired of the bar and returned to the hotel. I wanted to swim the next day, not to spend it sleeping either alone or with a pickup in my hotel room.

Playa del Carmen turned out to be exactly what I had in mind. The beaches were beautiful, the snorkeling superb, and the weather very warm. I stayed at the gay hotel Javier had recommended. My room was made to resemble a tree house, and was very spacious and comfortable. The hotel was owned by an unfriendly German, who had absolutely no interest in talking to me, let alone telling me about gay life in Playa del Carmen. He did not need to go out of his way to cultivate his guests. The next day, there were no vacancies in town.

Playa del Carmen is a playground for European tourists who fly by the planeload from Germany and Holland nonstop to Cancún. The scene was mostly straight. The beaches were full of bare-breasted European women. The only gay bar had closed a few months earlier due to a fire. If I wanted to do more in the evenings than watch television, I would have to cruise. In Mexico, invariably, the cruising takes place at the *zócalo*, the main plaza, where people promenade until late at night.

Twice I had made my home in Mexico. I have also visited the country dozens of times. I can recall only two occasions when I had sex at my partner's home. This situation is somewhat unique to Mexico because it affects the poor as well as the rich. I have written about this topic at length.[3] Unless I met a fellow tourist—unlikely, because Europeans usually don't turn me on—we would have to have our session in my hotel.

I prepared myself and the room with the precautions described in the previous chapter. I was not particularly worried about an untoward experience with a pickup (Playa del Carmen, unlike Cancún, is too small for really bad stuff to happen), but it was routine. After dinner, I walked to the plaza. It was a Saturday night, and the plaza was full of people. Children playing, teenagers hanging out, adults talking to each other, vendors selling food.

Going back to my first time in Mexico in 1957, I have paid for sex, either outright or as a "loan," about 80 percent of the time. I did not assume that on this particular night I would get it for free.

It would be highly unlikely that a Mexican hustler, in a small place like Playa del Carmen, would be brazen enough to name his price for sexual favors. I had to decide beforehand what I would be willing to pay in order to make a reasonable offer.

When traveling, you need to develop a feel for what is a just remuneration for a hustler in the country you are visiting. You cannot go by what you pay for your hotel room, because this is related not only to the quality of your accommodations and the general cost of living in the country, but also to how popular the country is among tourists, and how expensive it is to run a decent hotel in the place you are visiting.

But there are other ways to calculate a hustler's fee. For instance, if you take a local bus and compare the fare with what you would pay in your own city for the same service, you'll have a better insight into the local cost of living. (Provided public transportation is not subsidized the government.)

In Cancún, where the cost of living is very high compared to most of Mexico, the bus fare is one peso per ride. (About eight cents, as of this writing.) In San Francisco, a bus ride costs one dollar. I calculated that $30 (about 240 pesos) would be a very generous remuneration for a hustler. Had I lived in a rented room without air conditioning (as did my snorkeling instructor, a young Dutch woman), I would be somewhat less generous. But I stayed at a middle-range, air-conditioned hotel, and I felt that it behooved me to be more magnanimous with a hustler. Since dollars circulate freely at Playa del Carmen I preferred to pay this way. (Only two bills to tuck in my money belt.)

With hundreds of people at the *zócalo,* how do cruiser and hustler connect? Maybe *gaydar*—gay radar—does exist. It took less than fifteen minutes for me to connect with Armando. I do not even remember who found whom.

We chatted for a while. Armando was from the state of Vera Cruz. (Cancún is in the state of Quintana Roo.) I kept running into people from Vera Cruz, where unemployment is very high, who found jobs in and around Cancún. Natives of Vera Cruz tend to be darker than most other Mexicans. I have always been attracted to them. By my standards, Armando was quite handsome. He was a journalism student in his early twenties. Because of the economic crisis in Mexico, he came to Playa del Carmen to make some money. "Next week I will start working in a new *gay* hotel," he told me. He used the English word "gay," even though we conversed in Spanish.

"This is important for me to know. I am a gay writer," I said. This statement was meant to assure Armando that I, too, was gay.

Now that Armando knew about me, he said, "I have a lover. He's Canadian. He lives in Vancouver and comes to visit me a few times a year."

We talked about Vancouver for a while. Since we were out to each other, we could now start discussing the matter at hand. Armando, who lodged with a friend, had a convoluted tale about needing a place to stay on that particular night. I could have offered to let him stay with me, but that was not why he had told me the story.

"You know, Armando, I am sort of lonely tonight. When I was in Cancún I went to the gay bar there. I did not meet anyone I liked. So, tonight, I would like to spend some intimate time with someone I am attracted to, like you, and . . . I would not mind paying for it."

"But I have never done this before for money."

"Well, I mentioned this because it would allow you to rent a room tonight."

"Yes, this would help a lot."

"I can help you with $30. This is money I brought from home and have not yet changed into pesos."

"What will you want me to do?"

I assured Armando that I would not screw him. That could be done—in fact, it is done all the time even among "straight" Mexicans—but not without a liberal amount of alcohol. Since we were both admittedly gay, Armando could not have played the role of a *mayate*,[4] which allows a straight man to screw a queer for money without sullying the former's reputation.

"Won't I be taking advantage of you?"

I pretended to give the matter some thought. Then I said, "At my age, I should really know whether I am being taken for a ride."

"I suppose you're right. You seem to know what you're doing."

I took Armando to my hotel. I had become friendly with the night-duty clerk, a straight guy, also from Vera Cruz. There were no problems bringing Armando into my room. The room was equipped with a small refrigerator. I offered Armando a soft drink.

After some chit-chat Armando said once again, "You know, I have never done this for money before."

"Well, Armando, if this is a problem, we could do it for free. I won't mind in the least, and you won't have to deal with the money issue."

Armando started laughing. "You're funny, aren't you?"

"I try to be."

Armando took a shower and we got it on. It was clear to me that I was not Armando's type. It might not have been his first time to hustle, but he certainly was not professional. However, just as it had been between Jack and me, the first time was a challenge for Armando. He tried to do the best he could under the circumstances, and at least was affectionate. He was a pleasant enough person and, all things considered, it was an OK session.

"Tomorrow is my birthday," Armando told me. I have always been very lucky in Mexico in this respect. I keep meeting guys who have their birthdays while I am there. Some of them I have gotten to know well enough to ascertain that they were telling me the truth.

"How old will you be?"

"Twenty-four."

"Will you let me take you out for dinner tomorrow, in honor of your birthday?"

"My friends are taking me out for drinks. How about the day after tomorrow?"

We had sex twice more. Armando's performance deteriorated as the challenge wore off. He did not have a vocation for hustling. In my remaining days at Playa del Carmen, I did not meet any other partners at the *zócalo*.

I have written at great length about the trip and about Armando, only a so-so sex partner, for two reasons. Traveling to desirable places and having abundant sex experiences do not necessarily go hand in hand. Take Mexico. Abundant sex can be guaranteed in Mexico City, which is very polluted, unhealthy, and lately crime-ridden; also in Acapulco, an expensive resort with a polluted ocean. The more peaceful and healthier places, like scenic Morelia, Guanajuato, and Zacatecas in the mountains, or La Paz, a beach resort in Baja California, are completely unpredictable as to the abundance and quality of sex.

For me, Playa del Carmen is an ideal vacation spot. I like swimming and beachcombing. I feel at home in Mexico. However, there is very little for a single tourist, gay or straight, to do at night there. Having sex with an attractive partner to round out a day of swimming is more fun than watching violent B-movies in a hotel room.

A tourist, like a soldier, has to live off the land. For me, Armando was the only game in town. There were two ways I could have gotten it on with him—the way I described, by promising to pay him for his services, or by getting him drunk out of his mind and having a poor sex session with him for free. In the second scenario, when he woke up in the morning, he would be mad at me for having seduced him. I would be obliged to offer him some money to make up for his humiliation. Or he would want to "borrow" a large sum of money which, after having made love to him, I would not be in a position to refuse.

I prefer the first approach, which is more honest and results in much better sex. Financial well-being comes into the picture because I use my economic resources to make my vacation as pleasurable as circumstances permit.

* * *

I had a flight from hell back to San Francisco, arriving home at 3 a.m. By the time I went to bed, it was after four in the morning. When I woke up, at 9 a.m., I beeped Michael at work. A few minutes later he called me back. We confirmed our meeting after he got off work.

I spent the day unpacking and going through my mail. I was tired and cold. After my stay at tropical Playa del Carmen, the San Francisco weather was getting to me. What I needed to cheer me up was an exciting sex session followed by a good night's rest.

Michael arrived punctually at 5:30 p.m., and the pizza I had ordered for our supper arrived a few minutes later. When Michael sat down at the kitchen table, looking as cute as always, I felt a sense of great well-being. I knew ahead of time the good things that would happen between us. While we ate, I would tell Michael about my trip. He would talk to me about his doings while I was away. I would give him the little gift I bought for him in Mexico. An hour later, we would have an unhurried sex session. Michael would be as affectionate as always—probably more so because we had not seen each other for a while. After the leisurely and satisfying session, I would give Michael his $50 fee. Then I would drive him to the Castro and, by 9 p.m., I would be in bed fast asleep.

In the same situation, how would things work out for me without a Michael (or one of his colleagues)? Knowing myself, my horniness would win out over my tiredness. I would force myself to stay up until 10 p.m. and then go to a gay bar in the Castro. (Sex clubs are not for me because of the lack of privacy, and I would be too tired to drive out of town to go to the baths.) At the bar, I would spend money to buy myself and others drinks. I would have to listen to loud music I cannot stand. If I were *very* lucky, sometime after midnight, I would even meet someone who, more or less, appealed to me sexually. (Of course, he would not be a Michael. The latter, a perfect sex partner, had come into my life after a long search.) I would take my bar date home, or go to his place, hoping that he would be sober and that we would be compatible. Because of the lateness of the hour, there would be little time to talk to each other. With luck, we would even have good sex. Not as good as with Michael, with whom I am completely compatible. But, hey, my new partner came for free!

In the early morning, I would have to drive my partner home or return from his place to mine. If he stayed the night, I would have to get up early to make him breakfast and drive him to work.

The $50 for Michael was an excellent investment!

* * *

The thrust of this book has been to present hustlers as a readily available resource in the gay community. Unfortunately, it is accessible only by paying for it. Financial well-being is mostly about allocation of resources. I could, for instance, afford an annual cruise on a luxury liner with the money I spend on hustlers. For me, good and frequent sexual sessions are more important than two weeks of invigorating sea air.

There are lots of gay men who feel as I do. However, they won't allocate their resources to hiring hustlers because they believe that they should not do it—they ought to get it for free. My message is: Always try to find a boyfriend or a steady sex partner. But, in the meantime, utilize the services of hustlers. Sex is easier to come by when you are not looking for it compulsively!

Like any other resource, you need to familiarize yourself with the ins and outs of hustling. Do not be discouraged because a few experiences with hustlers did not work out. Learn from your mistakes. You will be able to hire better hustlers in the future. Last, as with any independent contractor, you *can* work out a deal that would suit your budget, your emotional and sexual needs, and your temperament.

Here's to your success!

Notes

Chapter 1

1. I have described my first experience in an autobiographical short story called "The Hurly-Burly," published in *My First Time: Gay Men Describe Their First Same-Sex Experience,* edited by Jack Hart (Boston: Alyson Publications, 1995), pp. 73-75.

2. For a fuller discussion of the opportunistic-hustler phenomenon see *De Onda: A Gay Guide to Mexico and Its People,* Joseph Itiel (San Francisco: International Wavelength, 1991), pp. 49-50.

3. When the AIDS epidemic hit in the 1980s, street hustlers lost many of their clients. Not only the ones who died, but also the ones who were too afraid to pick them up. (Of course, many hustlers died too. However, in San Francisco there has always been an unlimited supply of newcomers.) As a result, many hustlers combined their sex work with drug dealing. The street *itself* became a dangerous place for both hustlers and their clients.

4. *Pura Vida: Gay and Lesbian Costa Rica,* Joseph Itiel (San Francisco: Orchid House, 1993), Chapter 13, "An Interview with Ms. Universe," pp. 93-100.

Chapter 2

1. *Bay Area Reporter* (San Francisco), March 6, 1997, p. 65.

2. *Bay Area Reporter,* September 11, 1997, p. 61.

3. The out call—hustlers going to clients' homes when summoned—is a relatively new phenomenon. It could only have come into being when telephones became widely available, and service cheap enough to be readily affordable.

Throughout history there have been male whorehouses, with male prostitutes on the premises. They were much more the norm, at least in some cities, before the advent of the telephone. (Now there are model agencies that do referrals and take a cut from the model's fee.) Male bordellos go far back in history. Phaedo, one of Socrates's most famous students, had worked (involuntarily, as a war captive) in one of the many male bordellos of ancient Athens, where the philosopher met him. See *Sexual Variance in Society and History,* Vern L. Bullough (Chicago: University of Chicago Press, 1976), p. 113. There are still plenty of places in the world where one can find male bordellos. A few random examples: Amsterdam, Barcelona, Tel Aviv, Bangkok, Tokyo, Quezon City.

I do not intend to deal extensively with male whorehouses. The dynamics in a bordello are very different from the street hustling or "model" scenes—precisely because in-house whores are employees, not independent contractors.

4. There is nothing modern about hustlers performing only certain sexual acts or imposing a surcharge when called upon to do more. "A Guardsman [England, end of

the nineteenth century] might charge extra for taking an 'active' role in anal inter-course [taking a 'real liberty'] but would baulk at taking a 'passive' role." Quoted in *Hidden from History: Reclaiming the Gay and Lesbian Past,* edited by Martin Bauml Duberman, Martha Vicinus, and George Chancey, Jr. (New York: New American Library, 1989), p. 210.

5. I interviewed many Filipino CBs (the local abbreviation for "call boys") for my guidebook to the Philippines [*Philippine Diary: A Gay Guide to the Philippines,* Joseph Itiel (San Francisco: International Wavelength, 1989)]. In spite of their terrible living conditions (p. 50), and their abysmal poverty, the CBs were, in general, a happy-go-lucky lot. The real complainers were the CBs who worked in *casas*—male whorehouses. Their complaints were similar to those of employees everywhere: the management was screwing them. (A few complained that it was more than just a figurative screwing.)

In my time in San Francisco, there have been very few male whorehouses. However, there have always been referral agencies, which take a commission from the hustlers' fees. Here, too, complaints (mostly about favoritism) abound. In a whorehouse, the male prostitute, just like the female, cannot weave in and out of the job.

When a hustler ceases being an independent contractor, he gives up his freedom and becomes an employee. Though this might be to his financial advantage, as an employee he loses his freedom to be completely independent (and irresponsible, if that is what he wants) and is more likely to regard himself as a male whore, with all the prejudices this term connotes.

6. *20/20,* ABC, January 31, 1997.

7. Baths, sex clubs, and similar venues provide more availability of sex part-ners than bars. The point is that gays have places where some sort of sex is almost *always* readily available. Heterosexuals usually do not have similar facilities.

8. Arguably, the fact that hustlers get paid so much for doing relatively very little may not be good for them psychologically.

9. John Preston, a former hustler himself, writes, "Underneath the contempt that some people hold about prostitution is the strong pattern of contempt for sex. . . . If you believe that sex is good by itself without needing the justification of romance, then why shouldn't it be purchased honorably from a man who sees himself as possessing something worthwhile?" *Hustling: A Gentlemen's Guide to the Fine Art of Homosexual Prostitution,* John Preston (New York: Masquerade Books, 1994), pp. 26-27.

10. Hiring hustlers anywhere in the world, whether hustling there is legal, illegal, or in legal limbo, is never an inexpensive proposition. I suspect that it is the nature of the profession, not its legal status, that allows hustlers to charge as much as they do.

Chapter 3

1. In my guidebook to Costa Rica, I summarize an interview with male prosti-tutes in drag. One of them describes how many of her "straight" customers want her

to reverse roles. *Pura Vida: Gay and Lesbian Costa Rica,* Joseph Itiel (San Francisco: Orchid House, 1993), p. 97.

2. There seems to be a nexus between drugs and hustling. This is not a new phenomenon. For instance, a book published in Germany in 1926, describing the Berlin hustler scene, also mentions the use of cocaine among hustlers. *The Hustler,* John Henry Mackay, translated by Hubert Kennedy (Boston: Alyson Publications, 1985).

Chapter 4

1. There are plenty of young guys who are interested in senior citizens solely as sex objects. Theirs is a fetishistic fascination with old age. I wrote an article about this phenomenon. See "Dirty Young Men," Joseph Itiel, *Chiron Rising,* #66, 1995, p. 11.

2. The roles of "master" and "slave" are not always as rigid as they appear from reading the ads. For instance, the spanking hustler, once he trusts the client, may become the spankee. The sexual encounters between master and slave are choreographed to suit the verbalized and the hinted-at needs of each party.

3. A street hustler supporting a partner who is a poor wretch is not uncommon. Often it is a nonsexual friendship. It is almost like saying to the world, "You think that I am a loser? Just look at my sidekick."

4. Before the AIDS epidemic, hustlers would sell their blood or plasma on a regular basis.

Chapter 5

1. In theory, full-time street hustlers should not be lumped with part-timers. In practice, the situation on the street is too fluid to make rigid distinctions between these two categories. All too often, a hustler will fall out of favor with his social worker, for a real or imaginary infraction of the rules. By a stroke of a pen, the part-timer loses his status as welfare recipient and becomes a full-timer. A month later, with the benefits restored, he reverts to a being part-timer. This sort of thing can happen on a monthly basis.

Curiously, in very poor countries street hustlers are *more* likely to have a permanent home of sorts, however poor they are. Renting hotel rooms by the night or by the week are not viable options for them. They are much more careful about not losing their housing, abysmal as it may be, because it is irreplaceable. For a description of such living conditions see *Philippine Diary: A Gay Guide to the Philippines,* Joseph Itiel (San Francisco: International Wavelength, 1989), p. 50.

2. *Fag Rag* (Austin, Texas), Issue 97, September 27, 1996, p. 45. (Name and phone number omitted.)

3. *Bay Area Reporter* (San Francisco), April 17, 1997, p. 52. (Name and phone number omitted.)

4. Ibid.

5. Your eyes are the best judge of a person's age. Lots of minors carry fake IDs.

Chapter 6

1. Photographs are tricky. The only certainty about a hustler's photo is that it makes his ad more expensive. Some photos are a week old; others were taken five years ago.

Chapter 7

1. "Besides turning up in the most unexpected places, affection is promiscuity's main motive and its salient result" for a large segment of the promiscuous cruisers. *The Homosexual Matrix*, C.A. Tripp (New York: New American Library, 1976), p. 142. I have no insights at all to offer about gay cruisers who want anonymous sex *without* affection.

2. *San Francisco Frontiers News Magazine*, May 22, 1997, pp. 43-53.

3. See *The Miracle of Mindfulness: A Manual on Meditation*, Thich Nhat Hanh (Boston: Beacon Press, 1975).

4. The gay baths in San Francisco were closed in the early 1980s to prevent unsafe sex. This was done through legislation. A few years later, sex clubs, not covered by the same legislation, started opening up there. These clubs lack the intimacy that could be achieved in the private, lockable cubicles of the baths. In the San Francisco Bay area, only two gay bathhouses remain: one in Berkeley, the other in San Jose.

5. I realize that paying for bondage—and being in control of the scene—detracts from the loss-of-control fantasy!

6. "In some societies prostitution was believed to insure the preservation of families." *Encarta95* CD-ROM "Prostitution" (Microsoft, 1995).

7. This, of course, is a generalization. Some hustlers are extremely punctual, and are very upset when their clients are late.

Chapter 8

1. The baths in the San Francisco Bay area, before they were shut down, were very specialized in terms of age, ethnic group, body type, and sexual activity. The Berkeley steam bath had been predominantly black before it became a haven for all bathhouse habitués of the entire San Francisco Bay area.

2. "13 Years Ago: Liberace and Liberation," *Bay Area Reporter*, March 6, 1997, p. 13.

3. Lots of hustlers, probably the great majority, attempt to be secretive (regarding their hustling) as much as possible under the circumstances. I could easily write a book of short stories with strange and implausible coincidences that have exposed hustlers to the people they feared most. In this respect, the beeper, voice mail, and cellular phones have made it much easier for hustlers to operate their business with less scrutiny by family and roommates.

4. Being sexually available to all takers is not unique to gay baths and sex clubs. It was a cultic female and male practice in many ancient cultures. "The Hebrew term *qedeshah*, translated as . . . 'temple prostitute,' actually means 'a consecrated woman' and was understood to refer to a woman who literally made herself available to all comers in places of pagan worship." See *The Harlot by the Side of the Road: Forbidden Tales of the Bible*, Jonathan Kirsch (New York, Ballantine Books, 1997), pp. 131-132.

Chapter 9

1. For example, masseurs who confine themselves to a "release" massage follow, by and large, the protocol of legitimate massage workers. For instance, the length of their session will be around one hour because most straight massage workers do it this way. When the focus shifts from massage-plus-release to hanky-panky and release with a token massage, the session will be shorter because the masseur will make the release happen earlier. There is no protocol for sexual massages, because there are no protocols for sex workers.

2. A sexually charged ambiance is solemn. The pre-AIDS bathhouse orgy rooms were as solemn as a church. Except for the sounds created by various sexual activities, the packed rooms were eerily quiet. On the rare occasions when patrons needed to speak to each other ("Do you want to come to my room?") they whispered.

3. *Life Outside: The Signorile Report on Gay Men: Sex, Drugs, Muscles, and the Passages of Life*, Michelangelo Signorile (New York: Harper Collins, 1997).

4. This reflects accurately the cost of living. In 1965 I paid $100 per month for my furnished studio apartment. The same type of unit would rent now for about $700 per month.

5. In many countries (e.g., Mexico, the Philippines) it would not occur to a hustler to quote a price for his services. The typical Filipino answer to the question, "How much will I owe you when we are done?" would be *bahala na*—it's up to you. In such situations, I suggested, very diplomatically, that we agree on a mutually satisfactory price before having sex. It is not a good scene when, after having sex, the hustler feels that the client is not as generous as he expected.

All of this is changing because of the "global village." In international tourist meccas, such as Acapulco, hustlers nowadays (compared to a few decades ago) are very much at ease quoting their rates.

6. See *Philippine Diary: A Gay Guide to the Philippines*, Joseph Itiel (San Francisco: International Wavelength, 1989), Chapter IV, "Arman: Traveling with a Filipino Companion," pp. 48-54.

7. In the next chapter, I will discuss more fully what clients can expect when doing favors for hustlers. But even when it seems clear to the client that free sex should be part of the package—as when inviting a hustler to vacation in Hawaii—this needs to be discussed ahead of time. Don Leo took a model to Honolulu for a week's vacation. The hustler refused to have sex with him because, he said, he had assumed that Don Leo only wanted his companionship.

Chapter 10

1. The overall creditworthiness of individual hustlers varies even if, through services, they can repay the debt. I capped Gabriel at $100. I allowed other hustlers to borrow higher amounts.

2. A hustler who asks to stay the night, after having had sex, should be treated as a guest and not as a sex partner. If you feel that you will want to have sex with him again during the night or the following morning, it should be made abundantly clear to him *beforehand* that he will have to provide sex in return for lodgings.

3. I do not accept collect calls from hustlers. Some of them will even make local collect calls, about fifteen times the price of a regular call, because they do not have the change or do not want to spend their coins. One hustler called me collect from Oregon to send him a copy of a résumé I had written for him a few months earlier. When I refused to accept his call, he spoke to his mother in San Jose, California, collect no doubt, who called me (noncollect) on behalf of her son. To save hustlers useless calls to my answering machine, they can make collect calls, which I do not accept, to ascertain that I am home.

4. Gay author John Preston, a former hustler himself, thinks that exchanging presents with a client will send the latter the wrong message, that is, that the hustler wants to become his boyfriend. He counsels: "Give presents only to the kindly older men who have made it clear to you that they are primarily buying your companionship and that they would appreciate a gesture of friendship at Christmastime." *Hustling: A Gentleman's Guide to the Fine Art of Homosexual Prostitution,* John Preston (New York: Masquerade Books, 1994), p. 133.

5. A number of hustlers and models have helped me enthusiastically and voluntarily with my computer problems. (One of them, a self-taught techie, was hired by me to organize my computer files. I paid him the going rate for computer counseling which, at the time, was $25 per hour. He made $10 more for a sexual session!) I suspect that, unlike me, they considered computer work great fun. It may also be that it made them feel good to show a client how knowledgeable they were compared to him.

6. This is true of practically all hustlers who have boyfriends/lovers who do not know about their sideline. I often knew more about a hustler's life than did his lover.

Chapter 11

1. I have known a number of models who have professional jobs. They are so afraid of being exposed that they end up with a case of paranoia. A hustling arrangement with one person would be much easier for them to handle.

2. My question spooked Étienne. Most people he dealt with knew nothing about Haiti. As I got to know him, I found out that he would, at times, say that he had spent most of his life in France. I suppose that is why he insisted on the phone that I put an accent on the first "E" of his name. A childhood in Miami as the son of an East Indian father and a Haitian mother must not have been easy. But Étienne, Alfonso, and many other "ethnic" hustlers have a unique problem. Of a

hundred clients reading the ads, maybe only 5 percent are interested in them. But these readers, myself included, prefer them over all others. Had Étienne described himself as French I would not even have finished reading the ad. Whether they like or dislike their ethnic affiliation, it serves as their sales tool.

Chapter 12

1. *Life Outside: The Signorile Report on Gay Men: Sex, Drugs, Muscles, and the Passages of Life,* Michelangelo Signorile (New York: Harper Collins, 1997).

2. I have listened to a number of Public Radio programs on truck drivers in India. When they take a break at truck stops they will have sex with the female prostitutes plying their trade there. This is how AIDS in India spreads from cities to the countryside. Logistically, hustlers cannot have as much sex as a prostitute at a truck stop. In gay whorehouses, however, male prostitutes face the same situation as their female counterparts.

3. How can shy persons hustle? The same way that stutterers can sing. They become different persons under changed circumstances.

4. Often, the sex will take place in the vehicle—hustlers call it a "car date." I have never had a car date, so I am not an authority on the subject. This type of date (which hustlers like because it is short) is the least intimate and, to my mind, the most dangerous. The client, as the driver, is defenseless because his hands are on the steering wheel. The hustler, as a passenger, cannot leave a moving vehicle without risking injury. The sex itself takes place in public, an illegal act. Cars present all sorts of legal problems. Two examples: if a client's car is stolen it must be reported, and it requires a lot of explanations to the police and the insurance company. A brand new law in Oakland, California, mandates the confiscation of johns' vehicles.

5. In many countries the law requires tourists to carry certain documents at all times. In Japan, for instance, a tourist without a passport may be taken to the police station. There he will be instructed to write a letter of apology (I don't know to whom) and be visibly contrite. I'd rather deal with the law than with the loss of my passport. Sometimes, a photocopy of documents will be sufficient.

6. From time to time, there are attempts to legalize prostitution—a classic victimless crime. (For example, "DA Renews Plea for Regulation of Sex Trade," headline in the *SF Chronicle*, October 14, 1997, p. A15. In the meantime, however, San Francisco sends prostitutes' clients to "john school" to kick the habit!) Such attempts usually fail because of religious objections and opposition from neighborhood groups.

7. A registration document, including a record of medical checkups. Fingerprinting could be added to such a document.

8. As I have already stated in Chapter 5, the beeper has given models an anonymity they did not have with a telephone number. Phone companies check out service applicants carefully to be sure that they would be able to collect from them. Obtaining beeper service is, in many cases, a cash transaction. The owner of the beeper number can give a phony name and address. If he does not pay his monthly bill the service will be cut off.

9. The media reported that one of Cunanan's sugar daddies bought him an Infiniti and bestowed upon him a weekly allowance of $2,500 (*Time,* July 25, 1997, p. 34.). One wonders who was crazier, Cunanan or the man who gave him that much money!

10. In some cultures, and for some men, crime is more honorable than prostitution. These nonhustlers indulge in sex with great gusto, rationalizing it as a necessary step for carrying out their crimes.

Chapter 13

1. *Financial Well-Being Through Self-Hypnosis*, Joseph Itiel (Englewood Cliffs, NJ: Prentice-Hall, 1983).

2. Old habits are difficult to kick. I always run an ad somewhere. I am unwilling to admit fully to myself that, for me, hustlers are the optimal solution. Somewhere, there must be a perfect lover waiting for me! I told Michael at the very beginning of our acquaintanceship that, as soon as I find a lover, I won't see him anymore. I also told him that he needn't worry too much about this eventuality.

3. *De Onda: A Gay Guide to Mexico and Its People,* Joseph Itiel (San Francisco: International Wavelength, 1991), p. 86.

4. The *mayate* (from "dung beetle") is a "straight" man providing stud service—usually, in exchange for money.

Index

Order Your Own Copy of
This Important Book for Your Personal Library!

A CONSUMER'S GUIDE TO MALE HUSTLERS

_____ in hardbound at $39.95 (ISBN: 0-7890-0596-4)

_____ in softbound at $14.95 (ISBN: 1-56023-947-6)

COST OF BOOKS_____

OUTSIDE USA/CANADA/
MEXICO: ADD 20%_____

POSTAGE & HANDLING_____
(US: $3.00 for first book & $1.25
for each additional book)
Outside US: $4.75 for first book
& $1.75 for each additional book)

SUBTOTAL_____

IN CANADA: ADD 7% GST_____

STATE TAX_____
(NY, OH & MN residents, please
add appropriate local sales tax)

FINAL TOTAL_____
(If paying in Canadian funds,
convert using the current
exchange rate. UNESCO
coupons welcome.)

☐ **BILL ME LATER:** ($5 service charge will be added)
(Bill-me option is good on US/Canada/Mexico orders only;
not good to jobbers, wholesalers, or subscription agencies.)

☐ Check here if billing address is different from
shipping address and attach purchase order and
billing address information.

Signature_____

☐ **PAYMENT ENCLOSED: $**_____

☐ **PLEASE CHARGE TO MY CREDIT CARD.**

☐ Visa   ☐ MasterCard   ☐ AmEx   ☐ Discover

Account #_____

Exp. Date_____

Signature_____

Prices in US dollars and subject to change without notice.

NAME _____

INSTITUTION _____

ADDRESS _____

CITY _____

STATE/ZIP _____

COUNTRY _____ COUNTY (NY residents only) _____

TEL _____ FAX _____

E-MAIL_____
May we use your e-mail address for confirmations and other types of information? ☐ Yes   ☐ No

Order From Your Local Bookstore or Directly From
The Haworth Press, Inc.
10 Alice Street, Binghamton, New York 13904-1580 • USA
TELEPHONE: 1-800-HAWORTH (1-800-429-6784) / Outside US/Canada: (607) 722-5857
FAX: 1-800-895-0582 / Outside US/Canada: (607) 772-6362
E-mail: getinfo@haworthpressinc.com
PLEASE PHOTOCOPY THIS FORM FOR YOUR PERSONAL USE.

BOF96